THE KING'S BREAD, 2ᵈ RISING

COOKING AT NIAGARA
1726 - 1815

BY

Dennis & Carol Farmer

Illustrations By

Joe Lee (Military)
and
Marbud G. Prozeller

OLD FORT NIAGARA

OLD FORT NIAGARA ⸝
YOUNGSTOWN,
©1989

ISBN: 0-941967-09-3

This book is dedicated to the memory of:

Corporal Arthur Lyons,
late of
the 85th Nova Scotia Highlanders

and

George W. Heatherly

TABLE OF CONTENTS

British Officers, 60th Regiment of Foot, 1771

An Introduction

In 1982 Old Fort Niagara established a cooking program aimed at acquainting visitors to the site with the types of food eaten by the soldiers of the garrison. Period foodstuffs and cooking methods are demonstrated each summer by ladies in eighteenth century clothing. Perhaps the most popular questions asked of these women are, "Are you really cooking?" and, "You don't really eat that, do you?" The answer to both is yes.

In 1986 Mary Catherine Hallatt and Lynn M. Lipa compiled a cookbook for the fort which they entitled *The King's Bread: Eighteenth Century Cooking at Niagara*. This book was based on the research on food that had been done up to that time. It was well-received and very popular. In the time since publication of *The King's Bread*, new information has been discovered about the recipes included in it. *The King's Bread, 2ᵈ Rising* is not an effort to replace the first book but rather to expand upon it and include new research that has become available in the last three years. With many of the recipes we have included citations pertaining to who ate the dishes and where they were at that time.

We have kept the format that Mary Catherine and Lynn chose, grouping foods by the time period when they first appeared or were most commonly found. Many foodstuffs were eaten in all periods. Efforts have been made to distinguish the fare of officers from that of enlisted men. We have also expanded our scope to include the American occupation from 1796 through the War of 1812. This time period has similarities to the eighteenth century yet shows many changes and a greater variety of recipes. An index to the recipes, a glossary of terms, and a time line of foodstuffs are included at the back of the book for further reference.

The recipes of the eighteenth century were not as precise as those found in cookbooks of today. The measurement of ingredients was often vague or not given at all. Recipes were generally descriptions of what to do rather then step-by-step directions. The following recipe for "potatoe cake" from Amelia Simmons' 1796 *American Cookery*, is not atypical:

Boil potatoes, peel [sic] *and pound them, add yolks of eggs, wine and melted butter work with flour into paste, shape as you please, bake and pour over them melted butter, wine and sugar.*

The recipes included in this cookbook have been drawn from many sources, both eighteenth century and modern. Some were converted for modern ovens (and tastes) before we began; some we have adjusted ourselves. These adjustments were made to create recipes that work well and are tasty and attractive. For best results, you should use them as a guide and make alterations to suit your own taste. Cooking in the eighteenth century was creative and perhaps less structured than today. Be imaginative and remember at all times to be careful.

British Soldier on Campaign, 1759

Baking The King's Bread

Bread for the garrison was baked in large quantities. When Fort Niagara was first occupied by the French after 1726, baking was done in the *"boulangerie"*, now called the "French Kitchen", on the first floor of the "Castle". During the 1740's the French garrison built a wooden bakehouse separate from the Castle. This building burned in 1761 and was rebuilt in stone by the British the next year. The original French ovens were repaired and reused in the new structure. The 1762 bakehouse still stands at Old Fort Niagara.

The bakehouse contains a pair of brick-lined ovens. Each was heated by building a large fire in the oven cavity. Smoke escaped through the oven door and was drawn up the building's single chimney. As the bricks of the oven became hot, they turned a pinkish white, indicating that the temperature was high enough to bake. Sprinkling flour on the bricks was another way for the garrison baker to determine if the oven was ready. If the flour turned brown within three to four seconds, the temperature was right for baking. The coals and embers were then scraped out the door and deposited on the hearth.

Bread dough was placed inside the oven by mean of a wooden shovel called a "peel". The loaves were not baked in pans, but were placed directly on the hot bricks. Two doors, one wooden and the other metal, sealed the opening. The length of baking time varied according to the oven's temperature. Forty to fifty loaves could be baked at a time in each oven, and two to three batches of bread could be baked before the ovens needed to be refired. The garrison baker at Fort Niagara prepared one loaf per man per day - an many as six hundred to one thousand loaves daily during the British occupation.

Eighteenth Century Cooking Techniques

The types of cooking done in the eighteenth century were almost as varied as in a kitchen today. The style used would be based upon one's background and the tools available. The majority of cooking utensils were made of iron, tin or wood.

Although it might seem peculiar nowadays, most soldiers at Fort Niagara cooked their own food in a group of men known as a "mess". The mess usually consisted of five or six soldiers who shared a pot, a room (or, in the field, a tent) and cooking chores. We know about military cooking techniques and equipment from such simple orders as "An officer of a Company to see that the men cook their Kettles regularly every day" issued at Niagara in 1759. Another episode giving us a glimpse of early nineteenth century life was the 1813 court martial of Private Matthew Campbell. Campbell was sentenced to 10 "cobbs" (cane strokes) and two weeks hard labor for cutting Catherine Brown with a knife during an argument over a kettle. Private Campbell was frying meat in the kettle set aside for the purpose of heating wash water. When Mrs. Brown objected that it was not to be used for cooking, an argument ensued.

The kettle was a most versatile cooking implement. It was made of iron, usually as deep or deeper than it was wide, with short legs for balance. A kettle was suspended over a fire by hooks or set over a fire on a trivet. Kettles might or might not have lids. They are a very good choice for soups, stews, puddings, roasts and custards.

Next in popularity was the Dutch oven. Dutch ovens were used for baking single items or where a brick oven (bake oven) was not available. They were also made of iron, usually not as deep as a kettle, with three short legs and a tightly fitted, flanged lid. Dutch ovens could be used in place of a kettle for soups or stews. If they are used for baking, the oven and the lid should be preheated before the food is placed inside. A pile of coals should be placed on the side of the hearth, away from the fire, and the Dutch oven set directly on them. The food may then be placed inside the oven, the lid put in place, and hot coals distributed evenly over the lid. It might be necessary to change the coals several time before an item has finished baking. Changing coals allows you to maintain a consistent cooking temperature. If it is not possible to keep the Dutch oven away from the regular fire, make sure you rotate the oven so one side does not get hotter than the other. Another important hint for Dutch oven baking is to have an oven slightly larger than the item you wish to bake. The pie, bread or cake should not touch the sides of the oven, because that would interfere with the even flow of hot air within the oven.

Other popular eighteenth century cooking utensils were the spider and the reflector oven. The spider was shaped like a frying pan with long legs allowing it to stand over the fire. It was commonly used for frying foods, although this form of cooking was frowned upon because it was considered unhealthy. The reflector oven, or "tin kitchen" as it is often called, was made of sheet tin. It would be placed next to the fire where it could reflect the heat within its interior, allowing food to cook evenly. The reflector oven was popular for roasting fowl or making baked goods such as tarts and cookies.

When doing open-hearth cooking, you can control temperature by placement of the cookware and manipulation of the fire. Kettles can be raised or lowered. Coals can be added or removed from the Dutch oven. Reflector ovens can be moved closer to or farther away from the fire.

Cooking fires were started with flint and steel. Flint is a very hard gray or brown stone which will generate sparks when struck against steel. These sparks were struck onto a piece of charred fabric. Once the fabric had begun to smolder, it was carefully placed in a nest made of flax tow or unravelled twine. This would soon burst into flames. Finally, sticks and logs were gradually added to produce a blaze. Once started, a fire was kept burning so that additional fires could be built using embers instead of flint and steel.

It is important to be very safety conscious when cooking over the hearth. Eighteenth century women wore long petticoats. Fabric (linen, wool or cotton) could easily catch fire if it brushed against the coals or flames. It was not uncommon for a woman to die from severe burns because her clothing ignited while she was cooking. Fire was the second most common cause of women's death during the eighteenth century, childbirth being the first. A regular practice of the time was to dampen the hems of aprons and petticoats to make them less flammable.

With today's flame-resistant fabrics, clothing does not ignite as easily as the natural fabrics of two centuries ago. However, fire safety should still be practiced if you plan to do any open-hearth cooking. It is a good idea to keep a bucket or pot of water nearby. The water can be used to dampen clothing and douse flames. It is easy to burn a hand or fingers when picking up a hot pot. Cold water will help soothe the pain until proper first aid can be administered. If your clothing does catch fire, **DO NOT RUN**. Fire needs oxygen, and running will increase the oxygen the fire is getting and make it burn more rapidly. If your clothing catches fire, drop down and roll on the ground. This helps cut off the supply of oxygen. Apply basic first aid for burns and seek immediate treatment. Open hearth cooking is challenging and fun. Keep it safe as well.

The care of eighteenth century cookware is extremely important to successful cooking. Wooden buckets should always have water in them. This swells the wood and keeps the buckets from leaking or falling apart. Wooden bowls should be seasoned with oils to keep them from becoming dried and cracked. Wipe the inside with a cloth that has been dipped in unsalted vegetable oil and allow the bowl to absorb the oil.

A properly seasoned cast iron pot will enhance the flavor of your cooking. Wash the pot with a mild soap and dry. Apply unsalted vegetable oil to the inside of the pot. Then hang it over the fire or place it in an oven (at approximately 250 degrees) for two hours. Wipe the pot twice more with oil during the two hours. It is best to cook fatty foods the first few times a newly seasoned pot is used. Then use it for whatever you wish. Always use a mild soap to clean cast iron ware. Avoid scouring as this will remove the protective seasoning. Salt is a good natural abrasive for removing stuck-on foods. If rust appears on the pot or food has a metallic taste, it is an indication that the pot needs to be reseasoned.

We leave you to your undertaking with a little nineteenth century kitchen philosophy from Captain James M. Sanderson, U.S. Commissary of Subsistence:

Remember that beans, badly boiled, kill more than bullets; and fat is more fatal than powder. In cooking, more than in anything else in this world, always make haste slowly. One hour too much is vastly better than five minutes too little, with rare exceptions. A big fire scorches your soup, burns your face, and crisps your temper. Skim, simmer, and scour, are the true secrets of good cooking.

British Grenadier, 1759

To Provide the King's Bread: Logistics at Fort Niagara

The movement and supply of provisions to the garrison at Fort Niagara was a difficult and expensive task in the eighteenth and early nineteenth centuries. The needs of the troops had to be projected as much as two years in advance. This had to be done accurately and without delay, in order to give government agents time to purchase, package and ship the foodstuffs to America. Then, loaded aboard sailing vessels, the provisions of Niagara's French and British soldiers were transported thousands of miles to Quebec, subject to numerous delays and problems. The most significant of these delays was the cold North American winter which effectively isolated Fort Niagara each year from December until late April.

Once safely at Quebec, the barrels were inspected for damage. At this point they were often left open, exposed to corruption and theft by the quartermasters and laborers. Sometimes the load had been packaged in a container too large to be transported to the post. In this case, the food had to be repacked, at great cost and risk of pilferage, in order to continue its journey.

At this point, the "victuals" were loaded aboard small river craft such as bateaux and canoes, to begin the second phase of the voyage to Niagara. The containers were generally barrels, made of wood, and bound with wooden or metal straps. Barrels were produced in different sizes to contain diverse produce. Salt pork, the most typical meat sent to Fort Niagara (and eaten by all three armies - French, British and American) was shipped in 215-pound barrels. Peas and rice were transported in "tierces", each holding up to 531 pounds, and butter in "firkins" of 66 and three-quarters of a pound.

The bateaux were manned by Canadian boatmen or soldiers who were poorly paid and overworked. They propelled their bateaux and their cargoes up the St. Lawrence River, stopping to carry or "portage" the loads around the many rapids along the way. A simple trick employed by these inland sailors was to drain the salt brine from the barrels to lighten their load. Nearing Fort Niagara, they would refill the casks with fresh water to restore their weight and cover the ruse. Imagine the smell when the commissary opened the long-spoiled meat for issuance!

Once at Niagara, the provisions were stored in sheds and warehouses. One of those buildings, the Provisions Storehouse built in 1762, still stands at Old Fort Niagara. Placed on the site of an earlier French wooden storehouse, it provided shelter for as many as 7000 barrels of food. This was about one and one-half million pounds of provisions. The building has been greatly changed over time, and only its stone first story remains today. A cellar (for butter and root crops) and a wooden second story with a loft are now gone.

Victualing the French garrisons of Niagara, although a difficult task, was made simpler by the relatively small number of people to be fed. However, with the growing danger of a British attack by the mid-1750's, a greatly expanded garrison proved to be harder to supply. Today, we as yet know fairly little about French logistics at Niagara or the manner in which supply affected their plans.

The earliest French posts were established in the seventeenth century - Fort Conti in 1679 and Fort Denonville in 1687. They proved to be difficult to maintain because of the distance from French settlements on the St. Lawrence River and the hostility of the local Iroquois Indians. Fort Denonville was a much larger and more military post than Fort Conti. During the winter of 1687-88, however, its garrison of one hundred soldiers of the *Troupes de la Marine* were poorly supplied with provisions. Captain Pierre de Troyes and most of his men died from starvation and disease. By spring, only twelve survivors remained to greet a relief expedition. The French withdrew in September, 1688, partly because of the trouble of supplying the post.

In 1759 Fort Niagara's French garrison did not greatly fear starvation, a normal peril of besieged fortresses, due to Captain Pierre Pouchot's efforts to provision his troops before the arrival of the enemy. Indeed, in his memoirs, Pouchot recorded that the Iroquois allies of the victorious British "broke open and wasted all the barrels of flour" following the French capitulation on July 25, 1759, an indication that the garrison still had substantial supplies. Captain Pouchot also hosted a dinner in the French Castle for Sir William Johnson and a number of his officers. The gallant Pouchot was ill-paid by his guests when, at the conclusion of the meal, the British "helped themselves to all the utensils and movables" of the French officers' mess.

As soon as the smoke cleared from the siege of Fort Niagara, the new garrison began to face food-related problems. The British bombardment had left Fort Niagara in a sorry state of repair. The Flag (lake-side) Bastion was breached, buildings were damaged and earthworks torn down. Equally important, the gardens of the fort lay in ruins. The French soldiers, as at most colonial forts, had prepared gardens to provide fresh vegetables and fruit. The July siege operations had destroyed them. With military demands and the lateness of the season working against them, the new masters of Niagara could not replant the vegetable plots.

The six hundred British soldiers left to garrison Niagara soon came down with scurvy, a nutritional disorder caused by a lack of vitamin C in the diet. Vitamin C was normally obtained by the British soldier from his garden crops, as his ration of salt pork, peas, rice, bread, and butter did not contain any. Scurvy cost the lives of 149 of Fort Niagara's soldiers before it could be checked.

On February 6, 1760, Lieutenant Colonel William Eyre reported to Lieutenant Colonel Frederick Haldimand, then at Oswego, that his situation had become critical:

> *I find myself under a Necessity to Send off a Boat from hence for Yr Garison, by reason of the Increase of Sickness Amoungst the men; we have now Upwards of 100 in the Hospital, the most part of them in a dying way, besides more then that Number, which the Scurvy have broke out Upon, and very little of the Necessary things to help them ... I have been Obliged to Lessen the Guards near one half, but the Worst of it,is, I can have no Assistance for some time.*

The common scurvy preventatives in North America at that time were fresh fruit and vegetables as well as "spruce beer". Lacking fresh produce, Eyre tried to brew spruce beer. The "beer" was easily made with molasses, water and spruce branches. However, Fort Niagara was also without molasses. With scurvy striking 270 out of 600 men, the fort surgeon was forced to concoct another curative. He used maple sap, sassafras and hickory bark, boiled and served to both the sick and the healthy. Eyre hoped that this would slow the spread of the disease. Without vitamin C, however, the brew could not stop the disorder. Only the opening of the lake in the spring of 1760 ended the epidemic by allowing molasses and lime and lemon juice to be rushed to the fort.

From 1760 to 1796, the British at Niagara would plant gardens and orchards with seed provided from Europe. Crops included, beets, peas, carrots, beans, onions, cabbage, turnips and lettuce. The British were slow to accept potatoes as a foodstuff. It is interesting to note that they were not grown at Niagara until the time of the American Revolution (1775-83), but, by 1778, potatoes were being eaten by the fort's population. From 1782 to 1796, the garrison provided the chief financial support for the local farmers. Indeed, men such as Robert Hamilton, Richard Cartwright and Robert Nichol provided the commissariat department with flour, vegetables and Indian corn in amounts large enough to make them wealthy.

Fruit trees have long been associated with Fort Niagara. French accounts refer to peach trees grown on the ground between the French Castle and Lake Ontario (a space about 220 feet wide in the eighteenth century but long since lost to erosion). A report from Gaspard-Joseph Chaussegros de Léry, original designer of Fort Niagara, dated October 10, 1744, detailed storm damage inside Fort Niagara including, "that it had broken and uprooted the fruit trees." Fruit trees are known to have been cultivated within the fort as well as in the traders' village below the walls and in the garrison gardens east the post. By 1766, peaches were readily available, and currants, and cherries were grown as well. Captain John Enys, a British officer who stopped at Fort Niagara in 1787, reported:

> The Gardens within the Fort are not only sufficient to supply the garison with Cheries, Peaches &c, but also to send a good many to Cataraqui & Carleton Island. Indeed I have known Peaches sent from here to Quebec. They are surely not worth sending so far being very small and of little flavor but as there is no such Fruit in Quebec they go down very well and are esteemed a rarity.

The village between Fort Niagara and the river was known during the British period as "The Bottom" and provided homes to the sutlers and merchants at Niagara. These people sold to the soldiers of the garrison and traded with local Indians. A number of storehouses, stables, a brewery (for spruce beer), root cellars, and public houses in "The Bottom" provided Fort Niagara's residents with a ready supply of food, drink and goods not normally issued by the military. Also, having the merchants located just outside the gates allowed the commandant a measure of control. In his journal, John Enys stated that:

> There is no Public House or shop within the Fort they all being gathered togeather [sic] in what is called the Bottom, a flat peice of land between the Fort and the River, and all these holding thear permission only during the pleasure of the Commanding Office they are able in a great measure to prevent drunkeness amoung the men.

Enys found the taverns of the village to be more comfortable than the officers' quarters in the fort. Captain Jonas Watson of the 65th Regiment of Foot, then commandant of the post, offered a room to Enys, who declined "as I found I could gat a very excellent one at a public house in what they call the Bottom without the fort Gates." He did not record the quality of the cuisine, alas.

Fort Niagara never came under attack during the years of the Revolutionary War (1775-83). Its garrison, the Eighth (King's) Regiment of Foot, labored without rest building or repairing the defenses. The Bakehouse, with its two French beehive bread ovens, had been rebuilt in stone in 1762. This structure and other bakehouses served Fort Niagara well, producing the King's bread for as many as 5000 people per day in 1779. The strain of war upon the garrison and its commandants was almost overpowering. Projected foodstuffs for 1775 proved grossly inadequate due to the sudden addition of hundreds of Indians and Loyalist refugees. Stocks of pork and flour became dangerously low late that year as the King's men struggled to regain control on their vital lifeline to Quebec, cut by American rebels under Ethan Allen and Benedict Arnold.

The modern image of military life of two centuries ago seldom includes the numerous women and children found in every garrison. Each of these dependents was entitled to a half ration for a woman or a quarter ration for a child. Normally, six women were allowed to each British company during peacetime. These wives of the soldiers served the regiment as laundresses and cooks for the officers. At Fort Niagara, as in Canada during the war, the number of women per company was reduced to three. Even a reduction of fifty percent was not enough to relieve the subsistence problems of Fort Niagara. "Useless mouths" (the garrison women and children) were usually sent to Montreal and Quebec along with Loyalist refugees and American prisoners brought to the fort by Indian war parties.

For years before the war, British officers had tried to establish some means of raising food at the forts to reduce the costs of supplying the Great Lakes posts. It took the pressures of war to drive the point home. On October 7, 1778, Lieutenant General Frederick Haldimand wrote to Niagara's commandant, Lieutenant Colonel Mason Bolton, that:

> *The great expence and difficulty attending the*
> *Transport of Provisions to the upper Posts make*
> *it much to be wished that effectual means could*
> *be fallen upon at them All for raising a supply*
> *within themselfs 1 ... at least to lay a foundation*
> *of by degrees, supplying the Post with Bread; -*
> *And the rearing of Cattle is likewise possible.*

One of the most important logistics breakthroughs at Niagara occurred when the Commander-in-Chief for Canada, Lieutenant General Frederick Haldimand directed the commandant of Niagara, Lieutenant Colonel Mason Bolton, to provide tools and seed to a small number of Loyalist soldiers of Butler's Rangers so they could begin farms across the river from the fort. A survey of the settlement at Niagara, taken on August 25, 1782, showed that sixteen farms had been established by 84 men, women and children on 236 acres of land. The farmers, such as the three Secord brothers, George Field, and Isaac Dolson, produced 1808 bushels of marketable foodstuffs. The major crop was Indian corn, at 926 bushels, followed by potatoes (630 bushels). Other crops were wheat and oats. Hogs, sheep and cattle were also important with a total of 194 head reported at Niagara along with nearly fifty horses.

Indeed, the British government was concerned with "the great expence" of protecting and controlling the upper country. Lord George Germain, the man who directed the war in the colonies for King George III, found the posts of Niagara and Michilimackinac "so very distant, the Transport so extremely precarious and attended with such a heavy Expence to Government, all which might be obviated ... by raising grain and all kinds of Stock." Lord Germain told General Haldimand that "nothing is wanting but a Beginning" to such useful agricultural activities. The home government saw the cost of establishing farms as very inexpensive compared to the costs of supplying the posts from Europe.

The years following the American Revolution saw rapid development of the Niagara frontier, both in terms of population and produce. Fort Niagara played a vital role in providing a ready cash market for provisions. Indian corn and Canadian wheat became staple items on Niagara's commissary lists. Fruit, as noted earlier, was "exported" as far as Quebec, and the garrison gardens flourished. Politically, however, the days of British control of Fort Niagara were numbered. The Jay Treaty of 1794 dictated the turnover of the fort to the new United States. On August 10, 1796, the Stars and Stripes were hoisted over Fort Niagara for the first time.

American forces stationed at Fort Niagara from 1796 to 1812 were normally small in number - one or two companies at most, drawn from the Regiment of Artillerists or the 1st Infantry Regiment. The logistics of the new U.S. Army were simple and much the same as those of the British. Rations were composed of salt pork, salt beef, bread, peas, and vinegar. However, the Americans provided a daily ration of spirits, unlike the British who issued rum only for heavy manual labor or on holidays. The Yankee soldier could expect a "gill" (pronounced "jill") or four ounces of whiskey each day, provided by his "Uncle Sam".

Some changes in cookery came to Niagara by the Americans. Among these were a greater use of corn, whiskey and beef. These had been consumed by both the French and British but not in anywhere near the same quantities as by the republican troops. United States forces relied on Pittsburgh, Pennsylvania as a logistics center with great trouble and expense to the government. The Americans could not depend on the new farm settlement to aid them in their need to provision the garrison. Almost all the the new farms were on the Canadian side of the Niagara River as was everything else of importance, save Fort Niagara itself.

The American role in the story of food at Fort Niagara was more significant in the preparation of meals than in the introduction of new foods. Although the soldier's daily fare remained poor and simple, the scope of dishes available to the War of 1812 American was greatly expanded. Taverns and public houses dotted the American shore by 1812. Three in the village of Youngstown, one or two in the Bottom, and two at Lewiston, about seven miles south of the fort, provided a man with cash to spend many more ways to procure his meals. By the time of the War of 1812, two former soldiers of the American garrison had opened taverns in Lewiston. Thomas Hustler and his wife Catherine ran a two-story inn near the center of the village, while Isaac Colter's tavern was atop Lewiston Hill (the Niagara Escarpment).

Having provided some details on the logistics of provisioning Fort Niagara, the next chapters will deal with the foods themselves. The recipes which follow have been researched with an eye towards their use at Fort Niagara or nearby. The italicized references which follow each recipe are keyed, by author, to the bibliography. Each group of references includes the source of the recipe as well as contemporary mention of the dish or the food at Niagara or on the Great Lakes. The recipes are accurate and well-tested, both in the Old Fort Niagara cooking program as well as in many personal meals prepared during historical reenactments. We hope that you will enjoy this taste of the past as much as we have!

French Coueur de Bois, 1753

French Soldier and Indian, 1750

Cuisine à la Canadienne
1726 - 1759

Fort Niagara was established by Gaspard Chaussegros de Léry and a small detachment of soldiers of the *Compagnies Franches de la Marine* in 1726. The stone "Castle" and a four-bastioned stockade provided the garrison with a fortified and well-defended citadel. Within this stronghold, storerooms provided shelter for provisions and a *"boulangerie"* or bakery for the garrison. Officers had a *"cabinet au cuisine"* or kitchen in which to prepare their meals and a *"chambre au cuisine"* or dining room in which to take their meals. The enlisted soldiers of the *Compagnies Franches de la Marine* prepared and ate their simple fare in a *"corps de garde"* or barracks room, using an open fireplace and eating at their communal table.

The 1726 fort was the third at the mouth of the Niagara River. The first, Fort Conti, was constructed in 1679, as a trading post for the explorer, René-Robert Cavelier, Sieur de la Salle. This small walled outpost soon burned and was abandoned. Fort Denonville was the second post sited at the vital portage choke point. Built as a result of Governor Jacques-René de Brisay, Marquis de Denonville's summer campaign against the Five Nations of the Iroquois in 1687, this four-bastioned wooden stockade was home to one hundred soldiers. Provisions were stored in a wooden building and a bakehouse was provided for the garrison. Only twelve of the unfortunate men left to garrison the fort during the winter of 1687-88 survived to be rescued and withdrawn by a relief party in the spring. Fort Denonville was then abandoned and left to rot away.

The normal ration for the soldiers of the *Compagnies Franches de la Marine* during the early eighteenth century was three-quarters of a pound of meat (pork, bacon or beef) per day and a six-pound loaf of bread baked every four days. Other items issued were peas, at two pounds a week, and lake fish, often caught by the soldiers themselves. French troops hunted, trapped and grew food to supplement their rations in the years before 1755. Not all who worked for the government of New France received a ration, however. On May 24, 1753, while at the Niagara Portage, Captain Paul Marin de la Malgue, Sieur

Marin, reported:

> ...*that* [the crews of] *my 15 canoes had all been lacking salt pork for more then three days. Consequently, they have not had any soup at all and are not in shape to work for that reason; that is why I beg you to supply them with some provisions, although none at all are due them.*

Marin also complained that the barrels of salt pork were under weight. "Not a package, or at least very few of them, contains what is marked on the invoice," he wrote. However, Marin was dealing with a different problem than the English would later face. He found too much salt in the barrels!

The following brief sample of early Canadian recipes gives an idea of the flavor of early French Canadian cooking at Niagara.

Gagaitetaakwa (Boiled Corn Bread)
Common fare

1 cup fine corn meal (Indian corn)
3/4 cup boiling water
1/4 cup cranberries
pot of boiling water

Mix cornmeal with 3/4 cup boiling water. Form into a round, flattened loaf. Cranberries (or cranberry sauce) may be added for extra favor, a common practice during berry season. Rinse hands in cold water and rub outside of loaf to give a shiny appearance. Drop loaf into pot of boiling water. The pot or kettle should be large enough so that the loaf does not touch on any side. Boil for one hour or until loaf floats. A second method for making *Gagaitetaakwa* was to bake it, buried under the ashes, with a roaring fire above, until it is baked thoroughly.

This Indian bread was prized for travel by the Niagara region tribes and the early French. A very plain but thick and filling bread is produced.

Parker, p. 69.

Le Pain or Bread
Officers' & Common fare

2 cups luke warm water
2 tsp sugar (optional)
2 Tbl yeast
4 cups warm water
2 tsp salt
1 cup lard
6 cups stone-ground whole wheat flour
3 cups unbleached flour

Dissolve sugar in 2 cups of lukewarm water. Add yeast and allow to stand for ten minutes. Meanwhile, in a bowl, mix flour and salt. Rub in lard until smooth. Stir yeast mixture and add to bowl with 4 more cups of water. Mix well. Place on well-floured board and knead until smooth (about 10 minutes). Let rise in large greased bowl until double in size. Punch dough down and form into 4 loaves. Place each loaf out and again allow them to rise until double, then place in oven (use a greased pan for each if needed). Bake (at 350 degrees) for 30-40 minutes.

A soldier of the *Compagnies Franches de la Marine* could expect one and one-half pounds of *le pain* or bread a day. Sugar has been added to aid the yeast in rising. About four pounds of bread will be made from this recipe. This basic ration bread recipe is also appropriate for British and United States troops.

Hallatt and Lipa, p. 8; Sautai, p. 58.

Sagamite or Bouillon de Gru
Common fare

1 cup white corn meal
1/2 lb whitefish
2 quarts water

Boil whitefish in one cup of water and break up fish. In a separate pot boil corn meal (*gru*) in water until it takes on a gruel-like consistency. When this gruel is about half cooked, add the fish. Stir briskly and complete cooking.

The name *sagamite* was translated by Antoine Laumet de Lamothe, Sieur de Cadillac, founder of Detroit, in his 1718 "Relation" to mean, "a variety of things mixed together to be eaten." As the name denotes, many other things may be added to this "*sagamite*" to finish it. Meat, other types of fish and wild plants could be used to complete this simple yet filling meal.

Elizabeth Scott, pp. 24-25.

Bouillon Ordinaire
Officers' & Common fare

4 lbs beef
1 boiling fowl
2 onions
3 leeks
1 oz parsley
1 whole clove
salt

In a large kettle, add to 1 gallon cold water the beef and chicken. Slowly bring to a gentle boil. Skim with great care all the floating matter and foam until none comes up. Add the onions and leeks with the clove stuck into an onion. Simmer very gently. Remove chicken when it is tender. By the time the beef is done, so is the *bouillon*. This will take about 5 hours. Strain and cool. Discard the fat that solidified on top. This is a good soup as is, however, it is intended to serve as broth to many other dishes. Game, birds and red meat may all be cooked in this *bouillon*. Avoid using cabbage and root vegetables with this, but all other greens are good in it.

This recipe is included to provide a good stock from the period of the French at Niagara. It is listed, according to Barbara Ketcham Wheaton, in *Les Dons de Comus* of 1758. Since much game and wild fowl was eaten by Niagara's French garrison, the *bouillon ordinaire* is provided for the preparation of those dishes. At Niagara in the autumn, according to Peter Kalm, a Swedish naturalist who visited the post in 1750, "Both Indians and resident French soldiers from Fort Niagara are said to appear here [below Niagara Falls] daily to gather the supply of sea fowls [swept over the cataract]. The birds were said to make good food if they had not been dead too long."

Benson, p. 702; Wheaton, p. 208-09.

Baked Fish
Common fare

1 whole fish, cleaned

Make a smooth bed of hot coals from the fire. Cover the coals with white ashes. Lay gutted fish on ashes and cover completely with more white ashes. Finally, cover everything with more hot coals from the fire. Bake 2 minutes for each inch.

The natural bounty of Niagara provided much additional sustenance for the French garrison. Peter Kalm reported the soldiers providing themselves with fish and birds by collecting them after they had fallen over the great cataract. In a story of his visit to Niagara Falls, he recounted that "Sometimes, in fact almost daily, fishes suffer the same fate [going over the falls]." Kalm also described bear, deer and birds being collected at the foot of the falls. The commandant of Fort Niagara, Captain Daniel

Lienard de Beaujeu, reported that, in the autumn, his men lived on this bountiful crop.

Hallatt and Lipa, p. 22; Benson, p. 702.

Eels *aux Trois Rivières*
Common fare

2 lbs eel
8 oz butter
1 large onion or leek
2 shallots
1 gill sorrel or spinach (1/2 Cup)
1 gill watercress (1/2 Cup)
1/3 oz parsley
sage, savory and mint
wine or cider
1/2 gill vinegar
1/2 oz flour
1 egg yolk

Remove skin and backbone of eel. Cut into 2 or 3-inch sections. Fry lightly with butter and finely diced onion and shallots. Season to taste. Add chopped sorrel or spinach, watercress and parsley. Cook rapidly for some 10 to 15 minutes, then add enough wine or cider to cover the eel. In a bowl, mix the egg yolk, flour and vinegar with the eel's broth to make a sauce. Care must be taken to avoid curdling. Pour sauce over eels and serve. Dish may be eaten hot or cold.

After Peter Kalm visited Fort Niagara, in 1750, he detailed in his *Travels* that "Among other fish they catch are a large number of small eels of nine or twelve inches in length, and all the dexterity needed for their capture is to go below the cataract [Niagara Falls] and feel around with the fingers in the cracks, holes and crevices of the wet rock, find and grab them."

Syfert, p. 21; Benson, p. 707.

Fried Muskrat
Common fare

1 muskrat
2 medium onions
salt and pepper

Skin and remove the musk gland from the 'rat. Immerse in a
kettle of water. Chop and add both onions. Salt and pepper to
taste. Parboil until a scum is no longer produced. Drain off water,
leaving onions with the muskrat. Add more water and parboil
again until tender. Remove and fry as you like in a skillet.

Muskrat was (and is still, by some) considered a delicacy by the
French inhabitants of the Great Lakes. This small game animal
lives in marshy areas and has a strong but tasty flesh. The musk
gland must be removed before cooking, however. If the gland is
left, the muskrat will taste as if it has been allowed to rot! French
garrisons, including those of Fort Niagara and Michilimackinac,
have left large numbers of muskrat bones about their sites. In a
few places today, notably southeastern Michigan, the art of 'rat
cooking remains alive.

*Dennis Au, personal communication; Patricia and Stuart Scott;
Elizabeth Scott, p. 9.*

Boiled Muskrat
Common fare

3 muskrats
1 Tbl cider vinegar
1 tsp dill weed
1 bay leaf
1 tsp sweet basil
1 whole clove
4 medium onions
1 small cabbage

Remove head, feet and all fat from muskrats. Split hind legs and remove musk sacs from each leg. Also remove the musk sacs and fat between the shoulders. Soak in salt water for two hours. Wash until clean. Place cabbage leaves in a large kettle, lay 'rat on top of cabbage, add vinegar, dill, bay leave, basil, clove, and chopped onions, and cover with water. Bring to a rolling boil. Cook until you can just put a fork in the muskrats. Clean and serve. Afterwords, clean the kettle carefully to remove any aftertaste.

Dennis Au, personal communication.

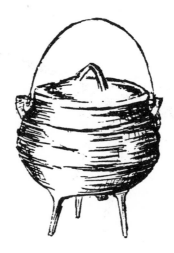

Potage de Chair (Salt Pork Soup)
Officers' & Common fare

2 lbs salt pork
vinegar
pepper and salt
2 lbs stale bread
2 lbs mixed vegetables (turnips, cabbage, carrots, parsnips)

Soak the salt pork for two hours in a kettle of water. Throw away water, and wash again. Cut into one-inch cubes. In a pan, heat a little fat very well, add cubes of pork to cover the bottom and brown well. Repeat until all meat is browned. Boil a kettle of water. Add pork and boil for 15 minutes. Add diced vegetables to kettle and cook for 90 minutes. Add a little vinegar, salt and pepper to taste. Cut the stale bread into two-inch pieces and add. Cook for 15 more minutes. Remove whatever fat floats to the surface.

Captain Marin de la Malgue, while supervising the movement of troops and equipment across the Niagara Portage, reported on May 24, 1753, that many of his *voyageurs* had not had any soup for three days owing to a lack of salt pork. He requested a supply from Fort Niagara. Marin evidently looked forward to the meal as he wrote on May 26, "I am very much obliged to you, sir, for what you have sent me to make soup with, and I can assure you it will be good. All these gentlemen will enjoy it with me."

Wheaton, p. 244; Winfield Scott, p. 7; Kent, p. 30-31.

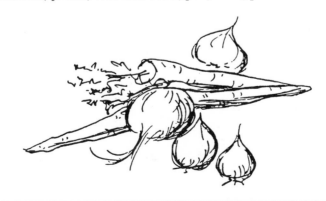

Biscuits de Chocolat
Officers' fare

2 oz unsweetened chocolate
8 oz sugar
4 egg yolks
8 egg whites
4 oz flour

Beat the grated chocolate, sugar and egg yolks in a bowl until thick and creamy. Add the stiffly beaten egg whites. Sift the flour over the mix and fold it in. Into cups place 2 ounces each. Bake in a moderate heat (325 degrees) for 15-20 minutes. Remove when the tops are just firm. Cool before serving. For a more eighteenth century taste, add black pepper and cinnamon in small amounts.

Chocolate has long been a misunderstood part of eighteenth century cuisine. This recipe was taken from *La Science du maitre d'hotel, confiseur* dated 1750. Surprisingly large quantities of chocolate are found in the accounts of the French and Indian War and later. At Niagara, references are given for chocolate as a drink used by many people. Some 40 pounds were requested for Butler's Rangers on September 9, 1779, for use while on campaign. While the manner in which the French used chocolate in cooking at Niagara is uncertain, this recipe was known and the ingredients were available. Another interesting chocolate fact, is that Indians, common traders, rangers, and prisoners were all listed as users of this delightful foodstuff.

Wheaton, pp. 262-63; Haldimand, Add. MSS 21760, Sept. 9, 1779.

The Manner of Victualing the Men 1759 - 1775

From the arrival of British soldiers at Fort Niagara, the importance of "victualing the men" was uppermost in the minds of their officers. Even as the British lay siege to the post in July, 1759, the proper feeding of the men was not forgotten. On July 9 General John Prideaux ordered "A man of a mess to cook the provisions of there messmate in the Trenches and carry it to them as soon as possible" and that "3 day provisions to be delivered out to the troops Immediately." To help keep his troops healthy, Prideaux also instructed that "An officer of a company to see that the men cook their Kettles regularly every day."

Having captured Niagara, the British then faced the challenge of supplying it. With the French soldiers' gardens in ruins, the new commandant of the fort, Lieutenant Colonel William Eyre, knew that his garrison would soon have to deal with the isolation of a long, cold winter without the fresh vegetables so necessary to keep an eighteenth century army healthy. Soon, scurvy broke out, eventually killing 149 soldiers of his garrison.

Eyre and officers like him took measures to stretch the provisions supply, improve its quality and lower its cost to the government. Nets were sent to the fort to allow the men to trap passenger pigeons and lake fish. A large quantity of garden seed was also forwarded in the spring of 1760. From then on, the garrison of Fort Niagara would expand its own food resources. A brewery for the production spruce beer was added to the trader's village, known as "the Bottom". Efforts were made to prevent waste, although these were sometimes extreme.

There were many problems in even moving army provisions to Niagara. A common trick of the Canadian boatmen transporting provisions to Fort Niagara was to drain the "pickle" or brine from the barrels of salt pork to lighten their load and steal the salt, "a very scarce Article Amongst them." On April 25, 1762, Deputy Commissary Neil McLean wrote to Major William Walters, commandant of Niagara that:

I find the Bungs of almost all the Pork Barrels
has been knocked out, & the pickle lost.- of Five
Hundred Barrels of Pork now in Store, there is

not above Seventy of them has any Pickle in them.

General Thomas Gage, Commander-in-Chief of British forces in North America, was concerned deeply with salvaging what he could of the spoiled salt pork. He wrote, on March 1, 1766, that:

I am much Surprized to find that Such Vast quantitys of Provisions are Condemned as unfit for any use, and must think if it had been more Narrowly Inspected into, that a great part of it might have served the Troops, or at least good Enough for Savages.

With the problem continuing, Gage ordered "that they do examine the Barrels from Top to Bottom." Unfit provisions were to be destroyed, but, "any not quite fit for the Soldiers, but which might do for the Indians it may be reserved for them, when they come to your posts." The troops were not allowed to be too picky themselves. "Nor are the Soldiers to refuse their provisions upon light pretenses that Salt is off their pork, or that the flour is a little musty," the general wrote.

The basic ration of the British soldier changed but little at Fort Niagara from 1759 to 1775. Tables of provisions allowed to one man for seven days 7 pounds of bread or flour (English flour, as the men refused Canadian and New York grain), 4 pounds of salt pork, 3 pints of "pease", 6 ounces of butter and 1/2 pint of rice. Sometimes the ration would vary to account for "overpluses" or deficiencies. Lieutenant Colonel Eyre, for example, was forced to make "An alteration in the manner of Victualing the Men" on January 26, 1760. With inadequate supplies of pork on hand, he issued 10 1/2 pounds of "flower" and only 1 3/4 pounds of pork with 6 ounces of butter a week. Sick men received no meat but got the same flour ration and 6 pints of peas with their butter.

The costs of supplying Niagara were very high. The normal expense of a soldier's daily ration in America was 4 pence per day. At Fort Stanwix (modern Rome, New York) it was 7 pence and 1 farthing. The cost for Fort Ontario (Oswego) was 8 pence and a half. At Fort Niagara, by contrast, the King had to pay 10 pence sterling to feed his men in 1765. What the British trooper did with his victuals was diverse and interesting, and sometimes even good to eat. Here is a brief selection of those recipes.

Three-Grain Bread
Officers' & Common fare

2 cups cornmeal
4 cups boiling water
2 tsp salt
2 Tbl dry yeast
1/2 cup water
1 tsp sugar
2 1/4 cups rye flour
2 cups whole wheat four

To make the "sponge", pour 4 cups boiling water over 2 cups cornmeal and 2 teaspoons salt in your mixing bowl. Let mixture absorb the water. Add yeast and 1 cup rye flour and stir. Cover and allow to stand overnight in a cool place. The sponge will remain flat, but the yeast will have worked. Mix in whole wheat flour and 1 cup rye flour, knead for 10 minutes on a board with 1/4 cup rye flour on it. Set in a warm place to rise until doubled - about 2 hours. Pre-heat oven (400 degrees) and shape two 9-inches loaves. Bake for 45-50 minutes (375 degrees).

Sloat, pp. 206-07.

Fire Cake or Ash Cake
Common fare

1 lb flour
water
salt

Mix the flour and a little salt (if you have it) with the water until a thick, damp dough is made. Mold in the cup of your hand, into a flat cake. Place in the ashes of your fire, atop a rock, if possible. Bake for half an hour or until blackened. Remove, cool and eat.

This delightful little treat was common to all soldiers of the eighteenth century when times were hard. Although the army would provide either soft bread or hard bread to its men, baking of often was not possible in the field or during a siege. The common soldier would then often prepare fire or ash cakes from his ration of flour. During the siege of Fort Niagara, Captain Pierre Pouchot received a report from the Indians that the besieging British were making these cakes. On July 12, 1759, he sought to use this information against them. Knowing that the Iroquois warriors were consuming a great deal of British provisions, Pouchot called an Indian council at the fort. Each delegate received a loaf of bread from the French commandant, and Pouchot told them, that "he knew that the English army had nothing to eat but flour cooked in cakes under the ashes."

Carol and Dennis Farmer, practical experience; Dunnigan, p. 49.

Stewed Eel
Common fare

1 eel
2 oz vinegar
1/2 pint milk
1 oz flour

Remove the skin and backbone from the eel. Cut into 2 or 3-inch sections. Allow to simmer in water for one-half hour. Discard the water and replace with fresh water. Add 2 ounces of vinegar and stew for a second half hour. Drain again. Mix milk and flour into a bowl as a cream sauce, add to the eel and bring all to a boil for 2 minutes and serve.

A second method, provided by Amelia Simmons, was to allow the eel to "jump in the pan" by not removing the backbone or cutting it into pieces. This expression derives from the characteristic action of eels cooked this way. Serve as above.

Soldiers of the garrison supplemented their rations by catching both fish and eels from Lake Ontario. Fishing nets and boats were provided to the garrison for this purpose. Eels were normally caught by placing some spoiled meat (something that the men had in abundance) in a cloth bag with a rope tied to it. After a time in the water, the bag was hauled to shore and the eels removed.

Hallatt and Lipa, p. 41; Simmons, p. 7.

Pork Chowder
Common fare

1 lb salt pork
1/2 lb peas (dried)
2 onions
2 lbs fish (whitefish, sturgeon, eel, bass were common)
1 Tbl flour

Soak dried peas overnight to soften. Mince pork and fish. Brown pork in kettle. Add fish, onions, peas and water to pork. Simmer for about one hour. Blend flour and a small amount of water into a paste and add to thicken the chowder. Season to taste.

By the latter part of the American Revolutionary War (1779-83), potatoes were being grown by Niagara's Loyalist settlers and could be added to this chowder. The soldiers of the garrison caught fish to supplement their daily rations. Fort Niagara's commandant in 1760, Lieutenant Colonel William Eyre of the 44th Regiment of Foot, noted in one of his dispatches that "We have been for some time past trying to catch Fish With A Net, of late we Are more Successful, which is of great Service to the Men, As I allow them ... to make Chaudre [chowder] With it."

Hallatt and Lipa, p. 20; Sloat, pp. 90-91; Gage, Vol. 5, March 18, 1760.

Venison and Rice Stew
Common fare

4 lbs venison
1 large onion
2 1/2 quarts water
salt
pepper
2 cups rice

Mince venison. Simmer venison and onion in water until meat is tender, about 3 1/2 hours. Add salt, pepper, and rice. Cover pot and simmer for 25 to 30 minutes. Stir and let simmer uncovered another 20 minutes or until the rice is tender. When done, most of the water should be absorbed.

Rice was a regular part of the British soldier's ration and was issued one day a week. The men of Fort Niagara's garrison obtained venison by trading with the Indians since they were not allowed to hunt. Turkey and bear were also brought to the fort by local Indians. These meats may be substituted for venison.

Hallatt and Lipa, p. 22; Sullivan and Hamilton, XII, p. 694.

Boiled Fish
Common fare

fish of your choice (whitefish, bass, sturgeon, herring)

Clean Fish well. Remove all fins and scales, but leave the head. Boil in water until flesh falls from the bones. While boiling, it will be necessary to remove the scum which collects on the surface of the water. The fish should be cooked 5-10 minutes per pound. When done, season with salt and pepper to taste.

Fish was a commonly accepted part of the soldier's diet at Fort Niagara and across the Great Lakes. French soldiers are known to have eaten local varieties. During 1757 the soldiers of the Marquis de Montcalm's army at Quebec were issued 2 pounds of codfish (probably salted) as part of their weekly ration. Patrick Campbell noted, in his *Travels in North America*, that while at Niagara in 1792 he "crossed the river to the north side to see the fishing, and saw 1008 caught at one hawl of a Seine net, mostly what is called here White Fish, and a few Herrings; ... I saw several other kinds caught here, particularly the Sturgeon, which is a bad useless sort of fish, excepting for isinglass, of which it is said a deal might be made here."

The British had eaten fish since the beginning of their occupation of Fort Niagara. As early as May 8, 1760, Lieutenant Colonel Eyre wrote to General Thomas Gage that "Our fish and [spruce] Beer helps us much, and I keep constantly men out gathering greens of different kinds in the Woods for the Sick ... The Net we have to fish with is very bad, I shall be well pleased to see that one you mention, which you have order'd up for the use of this Garison [sic]."

Hallatt and Lipa, p. 22; Langton, p. 147; Gage, Vol. 6, May 8, 1760.

Fish Gravy
Common fare

1 Tbl butter
1 Tbl fat (lard) in which the fish was cooked
2 Tbl flour
1 cup boiling water
2 Tbl vinegar

Melt butter and fat in the pot, add flour and blend until smooth. Add boiling water gradually, stirring until gravy thickens. Add vinegar and mix well.

A recipe for fish gravy is provided as a possible addition to the boiled fish. While we have not found a recorded use of this recipe at Fort Niagara, we feel confident about providing this gravy since all of its ingredients were easily obtained at the post. This recipe was also well know to English and New England seaport taverns for years before 1759.

Sloat, p. 86.

Passenger Pigeon Pie
Officers' & Common fare

6 pigeons (substitute Cornish game hens)
1 Tbl butter
2 oz fat (salt pork or bacon strips)
1 1/2 Tbl flour
2 cups broth
pepper and salt
3 onions

Put the "pigeons" in a Dutch oven (or baking dish) with your fat (a strip of bacon is best, though less available to Niagara's soldiers). Place the oven or dish in a hot fire (450 degrees) and bake for 5 minutes. Heat 2 cups of broth (chicken stock may be used) over a low fire, add butter and flour. Stir until smooth. Slice onions and add the birds and onions to broth. Allow to simmer for one hour over a low fire (200 degrees). Remove and debone the birds, place in a pie dish and add sauce. Cover with a pastry crust and bake in a hot fire (450 degrees) for 10 to 12 minutes.

Passenger pigeons were a popular meal at Fort Niagara and throughout early America, in part because of the ease of killing the birds. This eventually resulted in the extinction of the species and the necessity of substituting Cornish game hens for this recipe! The birds flocked in such numbers and were so docile that they could be netted or even clubbed to death. On February 12, 1760, Lieutenant Colonel Frederick Haldimand, then at Oswego, requested that "pigeon nets" be supplied to his garrison and that of Niagara. In 1773, Jabez Fisher, described "eating a hearty Supper of Pidgeons [sic] & Kildear [small shore birds]."

Common soldiers of the garrison would also simply boil the game birds without taking as much trouble as the above recipe. Elizabeth Simcoe, wife of Lieutenant Governor John Graves Simcoe of Upper Canada, wrote in 1795 that "Now the wild pidgeons are coming of which there is such numbers that besides those they roast & eat at present they salt the wings & breasts of them in barrels, & at any time they are good to eat after being soaked."

Hallatt and Lipa, p. 42; Fisher, p. 47; Gage, Vol. 5, Feb. 2, 1790; Innis, p. 165.

Mutton Pie
Officers' fare

2 lbs mutton
2 cups flour
1/4 cup chopped salt pork
2 eggs
1/2 cup flour
1/3 cup lard
1/4 cup water

Soak mutton in water for 1 hour before cooking. Remove mutton from water and cut into cubes. Place in pot with 1 1/2 cups of water and simmer for 30 minutes. Meanwhile, mix up a pie crust. Measure flour into bowl, cut lard into flour and work until well-blended. Add water slowly, mixing as you add. Divide dough in half. Set aside second half. Roll dough to fit baking dish. When mutton is cooked, drain off water and save it. Place the cooked meat in the bottom of the dish, layered with salt pork. Beat eggs with a fork and combine with broth. Sprinkle flour over meat. Pour broth over the top and cover pie with remaining crust. Bake until crust is a golden brown and serve.

A November 19, 1759, "Return of Sheep Rum Vinigar Beef Tallow and Candles in Store at Niagara" listed 81 sheep. The presence of these animals at Fort Niagara is confirmed by the faunal remains of sheep recovered by archaeologists. Captain John Knox also enjoyed mutton pie at a Saint Patrick's Day entertainment at Fort Cumberland, Nova Scotia, in 1759.

Sloat, pp. 82-83; Gage, Vol. 4, Nov. 19, 1759; Patricia and Stuart Scott; Knox, p. 294.

Roast Veal
Officers' fare

1 roast of veal (shoulder, breast or loin)
1/2 cup butter
1/2 cup flour
1 tsp salt
1 tsp marjoram or savory
1 tsp pepper

This dish will require a reflector oven for open-hearth cooking, or use your oven, pre-heated to 450 degrees. Spit the veal and secure with skewers. Melt butter and brush over meat. Mix spices and flour. Lightly coat the veal with the seasoned flour. Prepared meat is placed in reflector oven or on a rack with drip pan and cooked about 30 minutes per pound. The reflector oven should be placed 6-12 inches from the fire, and the roast should be turned every 20 minutes.

Fresh beef was sometimes available to the men of the garrison. This was most often obtained from oxen originally intended to haul carts across the Niagara Portage. A few of Niagara's officers kept cows, however, including Surgeon John Graham of the 60th Regiment of Foot whose wife, Isabella, wrote in 1771 that the eldest of her two Indian slave girls "milked the cows all summer."

Captain John Knox was present with the British garrison of Fort Cumberland, Nova Scotia on the 17th of March, 1759. The Irish-born officers hosted an entertainment for the remaining thirty-four Englishman. The party, held in a "suttling-house" (a military merchant's store), featured many dishes. Salt fish, parsnips and potatoes, "two buttocks of beef, 50 1/2 lb. cabbage, roots, &c." Other items included a leg of mutton, ham, two turkeys, four fowls, 54 1/2 pounds of "surloin" of beef, salad, "a hind quarter of veal", mutton pie, veal pie, two apple pies, cheese, soft bread, puddings (at 6 shillings, 6 pence a very rich concoction indeed) and 17 pounds, 11 shillings of lemon punch and mixed wines. "This festival was joyously celebrated, and with the greatest mirth and good humour," wrote Knox. It must have been a grand party because eight days later the captain reported that "Provisions of all kinds are now grown scarce."

Sloat, p. 42; Knox, pp. 294-95; Bethune, p. 5.

Rack of Venison
Officers' & Common fare

6 to 8 lbs venison
1/2 to 1 lb salt pork

Tie salt pork to venison and place in roasting pan. Roast in reflector oven or over open fire (325 degrees in oven) for 18 minutes per pound of venison. If salt pork is not available, baste the meat with butter throughout roasting time.

Soldiers of Niagara's garrison often traded with the local Indians for wild game such as deer and bear. Faunal remains in the Old Fort Niagara archaeological collection suggest the use of many types of game in their diet. Common soldiers in the 1760's are known to have traded with the Indians for deer, bear and turkeys. Farther east, at Fort Edward (Fort Edward, New York), provincial sergeant Jabez Fitch, Jr. "Dined at Capt: Durkes on Som Rosted Venson & Pickeld Oysters" on the night of December 19, 1757. Fitch and his mess mates often used their time on scouting duty to provide meat for the collective pot, a resourceful but dangerous method of rationing the troops.

Hallatt and Lipa, p. 42; Sullivan and Hamilton, VI, pp. 566-67 and 603-05; Patricia and Stuart Scott; Fitch, p. 38.

Roasted Turkey
Officers' fare

1 turkey (13-16 lbs)

Pluck feathers and clean turkey well, being sure to remove all organs. If means are available, stuff the bird loosely with a plain stuffing mixture (see recipe below). Spit Turkey on skewer (or place in roasting pan for oven cooking). When spitted, tie up legs and wings of turkey to the skewer to prevent their dropping as the turkey cooks. Roast turkey slowly (325 degrees), being sure to turn bird every 20-25 minutes to ensure even cooking. Roast until steam emits from the breast of the turkey. This should take approximately 2 1/2 to 3 hours.

Captain John Knox's list of food consumed at the officers' Saint Patrick's Day dinner at Fort Cumberland in 1759 includes two turkeys. British soldiers obtained turkey by trading with the Indians, and Old Fort Niagara's archaeologists have found 22 turkey bones in their excavations.

Child, p. 55; Knox p. 294; Patricia and Stuart Scott.

Turkey Stuffing
Officers' fare

1 lb dried bread or crackers
1 lb raw salt pork
1 tsp sage
1/2 tsp summer-savory
1/2 tsp sweet marjoram
1/2 tsp pepper
1 egg

Crumble crackers (bread) very finely. Dice salt pork finely. Combine bread and pork. Add to this the seasonings and the egg. If stuffing is dry, add 2 tablespoons of water to moisten. Stuffing should stick together, but not be wet to the touch. Place in cleaned bird or place in pot and bake at 350 degrees for 30-45 minutes.

Child, p. 55.

Indian Potatoes
Common fare

1 1/2 lbs Indian potatoes ("Jerusalem artichokes")
1 gill (1/4 cup) butter
1 lemon
1/2 tsp salt
parsley

Peel Jerusalem artichokes and cook in boiling, salted water until tender. Test for tenderness after about 15 minutes. Artichokes should not be overcooked. Drain thoroughly and dress with a mixture of butter, lemon juice (about 3 tablespoons), salt and chopped parsley.

"Indian potatoes", commonly known today as Jerusalem arti-chokes, were among the wild plants commonly gathered by British soldiers at Fort Niagara. Such foraging could be hazard-ous, however. In October, 1767, a soldier returned to his bar-racks with roots he thought to be Indian potatoes. He boiled and shared them with his messmates. Within an hour, two of the men were dead and a third expired two days later. The unfortunate soldier had fatally mistaken "thaspia" or "deadly carrot" for Indian potatoes.

Hallatt and Lipa, p. 21; Gage, Vol. 71, Oct. 25, 1767.

Pickled Cabbage or Sauerkraut
Common fare

200 lbs cabbage (or 2 heads for smaller appetites)
12 lbs salt (or 3 Tbl salt for the smaller batch)

Wash, quarter, core and shred the cabbage. Sprinkle with salt. Let stand 1 hour. Pack in keg and cover with water. Allow to stand for 6 to 8 weeks. An important note: if you use the larger recipe, the bung must be removed from the keg, or the force of the gas will shoot it out!

Reporting to General Thomas Gage in 1760 from Fort Stanwix (Rome, New York), Lieutenant Colonel Eyre Massey of the 46th Regiment of Foot, related that "As Ensign Bowden was bringing up the clothing, he saw Four Barels of Pickl'd Cabbage at the Falls [Oswego Falls], and as he knew his boats wou'd be the last, that wou'd pass, he took it in, I order'd it to be given out to the Garrison, and indeed told them there wou'd be no Charge again them for it, Cap[t.] Baily will inform You, the Men dislik'd it so much, that they wou'd not be at the Trouble to goe for it. M[r] Leakes Clerk has now got Orders to deliver it to the Men as Rations, I belive its not to be good as it smells intollerable." At Fort Niagara, in 1761, it was reported that "a number of cabbage had been thrown out of the Major's Cellar unfit for use."

Bowler, p. 54; Gage,Vol. 5, Jan. 11, 1760; Stevens, V, pp. 701-02.

A Pomate of Parsnips
Officers' fare

2 lbs parsnips
3/4 cup heavy cream
6 Tbl butter
2 Tbl brown sugar
1 Tbl lemon juice

Peel parsnips and cut into small pieces. Add the salt to a pot of water and boil the parsnips until soft - about 20 minutes. Mash parsnips and combine with cream, butter, sugar and lemon juice. Simmer while stirring often until well-blended. Serve on fried or toasted bread.

A "pomate" (possibly from "pomace", or "something crushed to a pulpy mass") of parsnips was part of a dinner served to British officers at Quebec in 1759. Parsnips were grown in Fort Niagara's gardens. They were popular because they could survive colder weather. Amelia Simmon's *American Cookery* notes that "they are richer flavored when plowed out of the ground in April, having stood out during the winter." Parsnips served as a good source of vitamins in the spring, when vegetable were scarce.

Wood, p. 33; Simmons, pp. 11-12 .

Hasty Pudding
Common fare

4 1/4 cups water
1 cup oatmeal
1/2 tsp salt
milk
sugar or molasses
butter

Bring a quart of water to a boil in the pot. Remove from the fire. In a separate container, mix a gill of water (1/4 cup) and 3 tablespoons of oatmeal together. Add the mixed cup and salt, stir in. Place on fire again. Add the remaining oatmeal a gill at a time. Stir to blend, and bring the pot back to the boil before adding the next gill. This should take about half an hour. Indian meal (cornmeal) or rye may replace oatmeal. Serve hot with milk and sugar or molasses and butter to taste. When cold, slice into pieces and fry in butter or suet (lard), until browned.

This English favorite was carried by the soldiers to each new post. A hasty pudding was a common dessert, thick and sweet. Figuratively, a wet, muddy road might have been described as "quite a hasty pudding" during the eighteenth century.

Sloat, pp. 144-45; Grose, p. HAZ.

Plain Cake
Officers' fare

6 eggs (4 large eggs)
1 lb butter
3/4 lb sugar
1 lb flour
spices (as available)

Allow butter to stand at room temperature until soft. Cream

together butter, sugar and egg. Add flour slowly, blending well. Turn in to greased baking pan. Bake (350 degrees) for 35 minutes, or until done. Spices may be added as you wish. Mrs. Simmon's *American Cookery* also allows for "1 gill of rosewater, 1 gill of wine."

Jabez Fitch Jr. recorded a November breakfast at Fort Miller in 1757 where "y[e] 16th In y[e] Morning We Eat Som Cake & Cheese & Drinkd Som Sider-" This plain cake recipe would be much as Fitch had. Mrs. Elizabeth Simcoe also described "those Cakes baked in a few minutes on an Iron before the fire which the people of the States make so well," as part of a refreshment offered to her for tea at Niagara in October, 1791.

Simmons,p. 62; Fitch, p. 32; Innis, p. 163.

Apple Pie
Officers' fare

4 or 5 apples
1/2 cup brown sugar
1/2 tsp cinnamon
1/2 tsp nutmeg
1 Tbl butter
1 Tbl rosewater

Peel and core apples. Cut into slices. Fill pie shell with apple slices. Sprinkle sugar, spices and rosewater over apple slices. Dot with butter. Cover with top crust and seal edges. Pierce top crust with fork, glaze with milk, if available. Bake in moderate Dutch oven (350 degrees) for 30-35 minutes.

Captain John Knox attended an officers' dinner at Fort Cumberland in 1759 where 2 apple pies were served.

Hallatt and Lipa, p. 33; Knox, p. 294.

Pie Crust
Officers' & Common fare

2 1/2 cups flour
3/4 cup lard
4 1/2 Tbl cold water
1/4 tsp salt (optional)

Rub lard and salt into the flour thoroughly until a handful of it, clasped tightly will remain in a ball. Wet it with cold water. Roll dough onto a board. Rub over the surface of dough and board with flour. Use just enough to keep dough from sticking. Roll dough lightly and quickly. Always roll away from you. Place crust in a pan and set aside in cool place until filling is ready.

Child, p. 69; Hallatt and Lipa, p. 33.

Whipt Syllabub
Officers' & Common fare

1 pint cream
1 cup dry white wine or sack
1 lemon
3 egg whites
sugar
nutmeg

Combine cream, wine and egg whites. Add sugar to taste, about 1 tablespoon. Grate in nutmeg and the skin of the lemon (grated lemon peel). Using a wisk, whip ingredients until they froth. Skim and discard froth. Pour into glasses to serve.

Syllabub was a very popular refreshment at "entertainments". In 1773 Jabez Fisher visited Niagara where "the gentlemen of the Fort being here treated us with the greatest complaisance ... Drank some syllabub, bid Adieu."

The common soldier, lacking the financial means to purchase

lemon and sack or wine, would instead use cider and milk, adding cream over the top of his syllabub.

Simmons, p. 32; Fisher, p. 42.

Hot Buttered Rum
Officers' & Common fare

2 gallons cider
1 pint maple syrup
1/2 lb butter
2 quarts dark rum

Mix cider and syrup. Bring to a boil. Add butter and remove from the fire. Add rum and serve. Do not allow to reboil. Makes about 50 six-ounce servings.

Rum was provided to those British soldiers engaged in heavy fatigue work. It was also stored in vast quantities at Niagara and was an important commodity in the Great Lakes fur trade. A very popular tavern drink in colonial America, hot buttered rum warms the cockles of the heart. This recipe has been well-tested at Old Fort Niagara where it is served at the annual Holiday Membership Social each Christmas!

Hallatt and Lipa, p. 48; Rex Patterson, personal communication.

Spruce Beer
Common fare

4 oz hops
1/2 gallon molasses
2 oz essence of spruce
2 oz yeast
water

Make essence of spruce by boiling young, tender sprigs of spruce in 3 gallons of water for 3 hours. Strain the mixture and discard the spruce. Add new spruce to kettle and use the liquid to boil it, again for 3 hours. Strain and repeat again with fresh spruce. Strain and save liquid essence of spruce. Take 4 ounces of hops and 1 gallon of water and boil for 30 minutes. Use only 1 quart of this liquid and combine with 1/2 gallon of molasses, 2-4 ounces essence of spruce and 4 gallons of warm water. Pour the mixture into a freshly cleaned cask and add yeast. Shake well and allow to stand 10-14 days. Do not place bung in barrel or the fermentation will blow it out.

Spruce beer was a common beverage of the British enlisted man at Fort Niagara and throughout North America. The drink was considered more healthy than spirits. Spruce beer, along with fresh vegetables and fruit, was also believed to be a preventative for scurvy.

The lack of spruce beer at Fort Niagara during the winter of 1759-60 was considered to be a major contributing factor in the death of 149 men from scurvy. Lieutenant Colonel Eyre reported to General Gage that he had "a Brewery going on here Upon a New Plan," but could not produce spruce beer for his scurvy-ridden garrison due to a lack of molasses. Instead, hickory bark, maple syrup and sassafras were boiled together to "make a very agreeable Drink." This remedy was not considered to have been effective and was probably intended largely as a placebo for the men.

Spruce beer was also used at Niagara during the American Revolution. Major John Butler requested 54 items of stores on September 9, 1779, to resupply his rangers. Included in the list among frying pans, chocolate, blankets, cheese, and blacking balls, were "12 barrels Molasses, 10 boxes essence [of] spruce."

Hallatt and Lipa, p. 18; Gage, Vol. 5, March 18, 1760; Haldimand, Add, MSS 21760, Sept. 9, 1779.

Chocolate
Officers' & Common fare

1 oz unsweetened chocolate
1 quart milk
1 quart water
sugar
nutmeg

Grate chocolate finely and place in an open sauce pan with water. When chocolate is boiling, add milk and return to the boil. Allow to boil for 3 to 4 minutes, stirring carefully to avoid burning. Add sugar to taste.

The *American Frugal Housewife* recommends nutmeg as a seasoning to improve the taste of chocolate. On July 5, 1785, while on Lake Ontario coming to Fort Niagara, Robert Hunter Jr. recorded in his journal that "By the greatest good fortune in the world two bateaux put up in this harbor [Isle Galot] with some cows and we got as much milk as we chose for a few biscuits ... afterwards took the opportunity of boiling some chocolate with the milk, for our breakfast tomorrow." On May 26, 1757, Sergeant Jabez Fitch Jr. noted of himself and his messmates that "we Cooked Some Chocalet and Picht our Tent and Had Good Entertainment &c." Only a week later, disaster struck. "Near 40 Cakes of chocalet Spild By Laying in ye Sun," Fitch reported. Listed among "Sundry Articles wanted for the use of Major Butler's Corps of Rangers-" at Niagara on September 9, 1779, was "4 Do [lbs.] Chocolate." Niagara merchant George Forsyth dealt in large quantities of chocolate during the American Revolution, although, as an agent for the British Indian Department, he provided most of his "chacolate" to the Indians. Forsyth lived and worked in "The Bottom", (the collection of stores and taverns located below the river side of Fort Niagara from 1760 to 1813). In 1780 he was audited for overcharging the government. The price of chocolate at Fort Niagara would appear to have been 8 pence per pound. Unfortunately, Mr. Forsyth was charging King George £1 6 pence (26 pence) for the same article!

Child, p. 83; Wright and Tinling, p. 87; Fitch, pp. 2-3; Haldimand, Add. MSS 21760, Sept. 9, 1779; Flick, p. 68; Forsyth, Sept. 29, 1780.

Tea
Officers' fare

loose tea
water

Measure 1 teaspoon tea per cup of tea desired into pot. Add boiling water. Allow to steep for 5 minutes. Pour into cups using a strainer to catch loose leaves.

Prior to the time of the American Revolution, tea was a more popular drink in America than coffee. Early in the century, the ability to buy tea was a status symbol, but, by the middle of the 1700's, tea was available to most colonists. Numerous varieties were available. In August, 1759, Captain John Knox made a list of articles available for purchase in the British camps near Quebec as well as their prices. Hyson tea sold for one pound, ten shillings, "Chouchon" for one pound and plain green tea (and that of very bad quality) for fifteen shillings per pound. Tea was on the list of supplies requested from Fort Niagara for the use of Butler's Rangers in 1779. Mrs. Simcoe recorded a 1795 visit to the home of Adam Green who lived near Burlington Bay at the western end of Lake Ontario. They treated his daughter, who was sick with consumption, with a tea made from Sarsaparilla.

Child, p. 84; Knox, p. 19; Haldimand, Add. MSS, 21760, Sept. 9, 1779; Innis, p. 184.

Private, British 60th Regiment of Foot, 1760

The King's Bread at Niagara
1775 - 1796

The years of the American Revolution caused a major expansion of the Fort Niagara garrison. The four companies of the Eighth (King's) Regiment of Foot, and a small Royal Artillery detachment were reinforced by other regular units and large numbers of Loyalists and Indian allies. The quantities of provisions required for a peacetime garrison proved to be woefully deficient, due to the rapid increase in people who had to be fed at Fort Niagara.

When war broke out in 1775, Lieutenant Colonel John Caldwell faced increasing demands on the provisions of his post because of the many Indian councils held there. One his most important duties was to retain the Indians' friendship for the British Crown. To do so was costly to the garrison's foodstocks since the King's guests had to be well-fed. Supply problems became acute during the spring and summer of 1775 as rebel moves against Quebec blocked the movement of victuals and reinforcements. Fort Niagara, as headquarters for the upper lake posts, also had to provide for the provisions needs of these satellite stations.

To make matters worse, many of Fort Niagara's ration items were substandard. The problem was due, in part, to the hurried nature of wartime procurement. Provisions contracts from Britain allowed personal fortunes to be amassed, at the expense of King and country. Contractors often sold flour "almost the whole old, musty, and sour: the oatmeal in general in the same state." Transporting provisions to Niagara caused even more problems as the boatman continued their old tricks of letting the brine out of salt pork barrels and allowing the flour to stand in water for long periods of time.

The King's bread, the mainstay of the soldiers' ration, was often the best part of the provisions provided to the common man. When the quality dropped, so too did the morale of the fort's garrison. A short "prayer" written by an enlisted man at Newport, Rhode Island in 1777 and preserved in the papers of British General Sir Henry Clinton, summed up the opinion of the soldier very well indeed:

Our Commander who art in Newport,
Honoured be thy name.
May thy work be done in Newport
As it is in York.
Give us each day our dayly bread,
And forgive us our not eating it,
If we don't like it;
But deliver us from mustiness and bad bakers.
For thine is the power to get wood and good flour,
For some time to come. Amen.

The worst supply crisis at Fort Niagara came in 1779. Although the provisions sent to the post in 1777 and 1778 were adequate for the demand, 1779 saw a number of events which forced Niagara to the brink of disaster. First, the 1779 supply fleet to Canada did not contain, by half, the quantity of provisions ordered. On top of that, rebel privateers captured four important vessels loaded with foodstuffs. The new Governor of Canada, Lieutenant General Frederick Haldimand, could therefore send only part of Fort Niagara's allotment forward that year. Also, the Loyalist refugees at Niagara had increased in number due to enemy action. Even worse, a rebel army under General John Sullivan was then marching toward Niagara, destroying Iroquois villages and crops. The Iroquois had nowhere to turn but Fort Niagara, which then had to supply them as well. As many as 5000 people relied on Niagara's storehouses during the fall and winter of 1779, and numbers of Indians died from malnutrition as a result.

Any war should be carried to the enemy's home country, and the officers of Fort Niagara sent large parties of Iroquois warriors and Loyalist rangers to wage a violent campaign against New York's Mohawk Valley and the Pennsylvania farming settlements. Butler's Rangers provided the bulk of the Loyalist troops at Niagara. Requests for stores for this regiment's arduous service in the field included many interesting items of food. On September 9, 1779, Butler requested a long list of supplies from Niagara's commandant. Among the victuals:

4 [boxes] Chocolate, 300 lbs. Coffee, 700 lbs.
Bohea Tea, 200 lbs. Green do [Tea], 30 Barrels
Brown Sugar, 3000 lbs. Loaf sugar, 60 lbs. Pepper, 3000 lbs. Cheese, 90 lbs. Mustard, 100 gallons Vinegar, 12 Barrels Molasses, 10 Boxes essence [of] spruce.

A post script added, "There will also be Rum wanted, if a greater quantity shou'd not be sent up, than has been already be done."

Fort Niagara's food storage buildings were particularly important, and subject to repair, improvement and new construction. An engineer's report of December 24, 1781, details the type of work undertaken by the garrison. From June to December, 1781, the troops constructed:

> *A root-house for use of the garrison, 50 feet long by 16 feet wide.*
>
> *A Provision Store new shingled, 104 feet long and 21 feet wide.*
>
> *A New Provisions Store ... 126 feet long by 13 feet wide*, for 900 barrels.
>
> *A small Room 14 feet square — with a fireplace for boiling Pickle* [brine for salt pork].
>
> *The Oven repaired at Niagara.*

In 1781 a number of Loyalist settlers began farming at Niagara, mainly on the west side of the river [now Niagara-on-the-Lake, Ontario]. This was part of a long-delayed plan by the military to improve the supply situation at the upper posts. Previously, the soldiers had kept gardens and John Stedman, the civilian contractor who operated the Niagara portage for the government, had raised a few crops as well as herds of goats, sheep, swine, and cattle. The establishment of the Loyalist farms, however, marked the true beginning of settlement at Niagara. Some former Butler's Rangers were set up as farmers, and, by 1782, their efforts had changed the flavor of eating at Fort Niagara. Large quantities of fresh vegetables and root crops could provide the garrison with its needs, even in winter. Gone were the dark days of 1759-60 when the lack of fresh foods killed 149 soldiers during a single winter. The period following the war also saw an increase in the varieties of foodstuffs and therefore the dishes available locally.

Niagara's role as an important outpost of the British empire began to diminish following the American War for Independence. The political settlement that ended the conflict placed the post on the American side of the boundary. Although thirteen years would pass before the new masters of Niagara could take up their station (again due to the politics relating to the 1783 Peace of Paris), the writing was on the wall. No major expenditures were likely to be made on a fort which would someday be turned over to the Americans. In the remaining years before the

British retired across the Niagara River, the garrison provided a ready market for the new farms of the southern Ontario frontier.

The ration of the British soldier of the American Revolution was little changed from that of the 1750's and '60's. The daily issue was one pound of bread or flour, one pound of pork, one-half pound of peas daily for six days and one-half pound of rice on the seventh day. The ration was supplemented by nearly one ounce of butter daily. Women married to soldiers and carried on the garrison rolls as laundresses received one-half ration and their children a quarter issue. Officers received multiples of the daily ration, according to their rank. This allowed them to support families or servants. A lieutenant colonel was allowed five rations, the major four, each captain three, and each lieutenant and ensign two.

Soldiers could trade, buy or barter for other foods and grow their own vegetables in order to supplement the ration. Smaller quantities of game were eaten by the British than by the French, and the post-Revolutionary War garrison could find even less wild food as settlement increased and the supply of game was depleted. Moreover, British soldiers were not allowed to hunt with their muskets. This prevented wear and tear on the King's arms. It also prevented hunters from alarming the fort's sentries. Equally important, this policy made desertion more difficult, as an armed man had a greater chance of surviving in the wilderness. Here are a number of recipes relating to the 1775 to 1796 time period.

Rusks
Officers' fare

1/4 lb butter
1 cup milk
7 eggs
6 Tbl sugar
1 package dry yeast (a modern expedient)
3 cups rye flour
3 cups whole wheat flour

Beat the eggs in a mixing bowl. Add 1/2 cup milk, and 1/4 lb. melted butter. Add yeast, sugar and 3 cups flour. Stir for 2 to 3 minutes. Allow to rise for 1/2 hour in a warm place. Add remaining 3 cups of flour and work it in well - stiff, but not too stiff. Divide into about 2 dozen cakes each about 3-4 inches in diameter and flattened. Fry on a heavy, greased skillet for about 7 minutes. Watch to avoid burning. Flip and press down, cook 7 minutes and serve hot with butter.

While on a journey to Fort Niagara, Robert Hunter Jr., a young London merchant, enjoyed rusks at breakfast on a number of occasions such as Sunday, July 3, 1785. "We breakfasted very heartily at seven o'clock this morning on cold beef, rusk and butter, and wine and water. It did me an amazing deal of good," he recorded in his diary.

Sloat, pp. 210-11; Wright and Tinling, p. 80.

Flummery
Common fare

oatmeal
water

Mix the oatmeal into the water and place in a kettle. Bring to a rolling boil until the oatmeal reaches a "jelly-like" state.

Served to the sick in hospital and to other poor people, "flummery" was also slang for a flattering compliment. Neither were found to be overly nourishing. In his 1780 publication, *The Regulator*, Thomas Simes provided "Instruction to Form the Officer and Complete the Soldier." He recommended, as a diet for the sick, "water-gruel" for breakfast, 4 ounces of boiled beef and a pint of broth for dinner and a pint of broth or gruel for supper.

Grose, p. FLY; Simes, pp. 82-83.

Bubble and Squeak
Common fare

2 lbs beef
2 lbs cabbage (a small head)
1 tsp vinegar

Take the beef, boiled or roasted, and cut into bite-size pieces. Boil a small head of cabbage. Cool and chop the cabbage into small bits. Add both together in the kettle with a little water. Add salt and pepper as needed. Keep stirring until hot. Add vinegar to broth before serving.

Bubble and squeak was another popular dish of British and American troops and was used as late as the Civil War. The name of this dish was derived from the sound it makes while cooking. The cabbage was obtained by British soldiers from their own gardens. It was grown from government seed, sent from England.

Syfert, p. 13; Grose, p. BUD.

A Michilimackinac Stew
Officers' fare

2 lbs beef
1/2 cup corn (Indian corn)
1/2 cup peas
4 medium potatoes
2 Tbl flour

Debone and dice beef. Brown the meat thoroughly. Peel (if desired) and dice potatoes. Place beef, potatoes and peas in pot and cover with water. Dissolve flour into 1 cup of water and add to pot. Allow to simmer about 45 minutes or until gravy begins to thicken. Add corn and cook for 20 more minutes.

Fort Michilimackinac Barracksmaster John Askin and his family ate this stew between 1774 and 1779. Askin, who was also a merchant, could afford a higher standard of foodstuffs than the common soldier. He even had an Indian slave or *"panis"* named Charlotte to serve as cook so that his wife, Archange, was spared this necessary but dull task.

Armour and Widder, p. 37.

Veal Cutlets
Common fare

1 1/2 lbs veal
2 egg whites
3/4 cups dried bread crumbs
1/4 cup butter or bacon fat

Slice veal into thin (1/4 inch) strips. Beat egg whites in a shallow bowl. Spread bread crumbs in another bowl. Dip each strip of veal into the egg whites and coat with crumbs. Melt fat in a spider (skillet) and fry meat for 3 to 4 minutes until browned. Turn and fry other side.

Mrs. Elizabeth Simcoe related that her cook could also make "veal cutlets" out of fresh sturgeon. "Cooks who know how to dress parts of them cutting away all that is oily & strong, make excellent dishes from Sturgeon such as mock turtle soup, Veal Cutlets & it is very good roasted with bread crumbs, she wrote in 1792.

Sloat, p. 45; Innis, p. 81.

Ration Stew
Common fare

1 lb salt pork (fresh pork may be used to suit modern tastes)
1/2 lb dried peas and/or rice
fresh or dried vegetables according to season

Brown the salt pork and cook in a pot of water for one-half hour. If using peas, let them soak in water ahead of time until they swell. Dried peas take longer to cook than do fresh peas, so they should be added to the pot at the same time as the pork. If using rice, add it directly to the boiling water to avoid clumping. Fresh or dried vegetables should be added later. Simmer until done - about 2-3 hours. Herbs and spices such as parsley, thyme and rosemary could be added from the fort's gardens to as flavoring.

The simple ration stew was the staple meal for the common soldier throughout the British occupation of Fort Niagara. This meal was easy to prepare and made the most of the foodstuffs at hand. The men could add any number of items to this basic dish, and it did not spoil quickly. Known to modern Old Fort Niagara Guardsmen as the "Green Death".

Hallatt and Lipa,p. 19.

Salmon-Gundy
Officers' & Common fare

2 apples
2 onions
2 lbs veal or chicken
1/2 lb pickled herring
1 oz oil
1 oz vinegar

Take apples, onions and pickled herring, mince finely and place in a bowl. Prepare and cook your veal or chicken (boned chicken) and place in a bowl. Mix oil and vinegar together as a dressing and add seasoning to taste. Serve as you like it (*"selon mon goust"*).

This dish was perhaps named after the French phrase *"selon mon goust"* (roughly, "as you like it"), but is more likely named after the Countess of Salmagondi, lady in waiting to Queen Mary, wife of King Henri IV of France. Long popular in English cookery, this was a favorite of inns and taverns. This recipe was popular enough to be included in *A Classical Dictionary of the Vulgar Tongue* of 1785.

Grose, p. SCA.

Rice
Common fare

4 oz rice (brown long grain)
2 cups water
salt, pepper and butter

Bring water to a boil, add rice and cover tightly. Boil until tender and water is absorbed, about 15 minutes. Season to taste with salt, pepper and butter. British soldiers at Fort Niagara could expect eight ounces of rice per week, issued each Tuesday and

Saturday in one-gill lots.

Sergeant Jabez Fitch, Jr. described that, as provisions ran low near Lake George, New York in 1759, that he was forced to cook his rice without sweetening, butter or salt, but that it tasted very good. Rice remained an item of issue at Fort Niagara until British soldiers withdrew in 1796. United States troops continued to eat rice, but it was not a regular ration item.

Fitch, p. 2.

Kedgeree
Common fare

3 cups dried peas
1 1/2 cups rice
6 cups water
3/4 tsp ginger
salt and pepper
parsley
1 onion
1 hard boiled egg

Soak dried peas overnight. Drain water. Add rice and the 6 cups of water. Cook for 2 hours, then add ginger, salt and pepper to taste. Cook for 1 or 2 hours until the kedgeree has a thick consistency. Cut onion into rings and fry. Slice egg into rings as well. Garnish dish with parsley, fried onion and egg.

A simple and more imaginative use of a soldier's rations and the garrison's garden would provide such dishes as kedgeree, which would, however, remain uncommon to the enlisted man's diet.

Hallatt and Lipa, p. 20.

Pease Soup
Officers' & Common fare

1/2 lb split peas
1/4 salt pork
1 meaty ham bone
1 medium onion, diced
1/2 cup carrots, diced
1/2 tsp dry mustard
1/8 tsp savory
3 whole cloves
salt and pepper

Cover peas with four inches of water. Add other ingredients and bring to a boil. Reduce heat and allow to simmer for two hours or until peas are cooked.

This recipe is much better then the ration stew or "pease soup" the common soldier would normally have eaten. However, people with more means or access to other sources of foodstuffs, such as a merchant or trader, could enjoy this much more tasty dish. Mrs. Simcoe reported in 1793 that "The leaves dried [Oswego bitter] are good in peas soup or forced meat." She also recorded that same day that she had missed a meal the week before but had "some of the excellent New York biscuits which I eat & said nothing about my dinner, feeling a pleasure in being able to be independent." Robert Hunter, Jr. also recorded a meal of "good pea soup and sturgeon," along with a kettle of fresh milk, eaten with his boatmen, in 1785.

Hallatt and Lipa, p. 12; Innis, p. 99; Wright and Tinling, p. 69.

Roasted Potatoes
Officers' & Common fare

1-2 medium potatoes (per person)

Choose potatoes of about the same size. Wash thoroughly and peel. Place in boiling water for 10-15 minutes. Drain water and place under a roast of meat already mostly cooked. Baste with juice from the roast and cook potatoes 15-20 minutes on each side. Serve on platter with roast or in a separate bowl.

In his travels upon Lake Erie near Buffalo Creek in 1796, Isaac Weld, Jr. "found two farm houses, adjoining about thirty acres of cleared land. At one of these we procured a couple of sheep, some fowls, and a quantity of potatoes, to add to our store of provisions." Weld and his travelling companions had a meal prepared for them by the "old woman of the house," which consisted of coarse "cake bread, roasted potatoes, and bear's flesh salted, which last we found by no means unpalatable." The above recipe may indeed be used with "bear's flesh salted," but beef or other meats may be easier to obtain.

Sloat, p. 115; Weld, pp. 149-50.

Sallet (or Salad)
Officers' & Common fare

scallions
radishes
lettuce
cabbage
cucumber
carrots, cooked
turnips, cooked
onions, cooked
beans, cooked
asparagus, cooked
vinegar
sallet-oyle (salad oil)
sugar (optional)

Shred cabbage and lettuce. Slice radishes, scallions, cucumbers and cooked vegetables. Mix together. Dress with vinegar and oil. Add sugar to dressing for taste if desired.

Jabez Fisher, an adventurous Philadelphian travelling between the British forts in the Colony of New York during the summer of 1773, noted in his diary that "we went up to the Fort [Fort Ontario at Oswego], got some potatoes, sallad and milk." There were also vegetable gardens at Fort Niagara. However, it is likely that Fisher's "sallets" were simpler than the one listed above and most likely only part of the diet of an officer.

Fisher, p. 49.

Gingerbread
Officers' fare

2 1/2 cups flour
1 cup molasses
1 tsp baking soda (substitute for the original pearl ash - see glossary)
1/3 cup boiling water
1 tsp ginger
1/3 cup butter
1/2 tsp cinnamon

Combine flour, ginger, cinnamon, and baking soda in a bowl. In a separate bowl, add molasses and butter to the boiling water. Stir into this the dry ingredients. Knead dough until it is stiff. Set aside in a cold place until dough is thoroughly chilled (approximately 15 minutes). Roll out dough on floured board. Bake in hot dutch oven (350 degrees) for 15 minutes or in a brick oven or tin kitchen for 10-12 minutes.

Gingerbread was very popular in England and was brought to the colonies by immigrants and soldiers alike. *A Classical Dictionary of the Vulgar Tongue* of 1785 describes "Gingerbread. A cake made of treacle, flour and grated ginger; also money. He has the gingerbread; he is rich."

Child, p. 70; Simmons, p. 36; Grose, p. GIZ.

Tarts
Officers' fare

2 eggs
1/2 cup cold water
3/4 lb butter
1 lb flour
fresh fruit (or dried fruit, out of season)
sugar
nutmeg, cloves and cinnamon

To make the pastry, separate egg yolks from whites and set aside. Whip egg whites until frothy, but not stiff. Add to the whites, 1/2 cup cold water and 1 egg yolk, discarding the other yolk. Blend together until it forms a smooth paste. In another bowl add flour and softened butter. Mix together until smooth. Combine egg whites with flour mix, one-half cup at a time, blending thoroughly each time until it forms a dough. Roll pastry dough out into a one quarter-inch thick sheet and cut out into cup-sized sections. Set aside to await the filling. To make the filling, peel, slice, wash, and pit the fruit as necessary. Cook fruit until soft. Strain off excess water and sweeten to taste. Place fruit into center of pastry, fold over and bake (400 degrees) for 8-10 minutes. Fruits suggested for filling, available at Fort Niagara in the eighteenth century were:

apples, blackberries, cherries, cranberries,
currants, peaches, hurtleberries,
may apples, pears, raspberries, and strawberries.

Mrs. Elizabeth Simcoe's diary for July, 2, 1793, records, "We treated them with Cherries. The Indians are particularly fond of fruit. We have 30 large May Duke Cherry trees behind the house & 3 standard Peach trees which supplied us last autumn for Tarts & Deserts during 6 weeks besides the numbers the young men ate."

Simmons, pp. 55-57; Child, p. 69; Innis, p. 97.

Peach Pie
Officers' fare

approximately 15 peaches
1 egg
2 Tbl flour
2/3 cup brown sugar
1/3 cup butter
1/2 tsp cinnamon
1/2 tsp nutmeg

Peel and pit peaches. Cut into slices. Fill pie crust with sliced peaches. Combine egg, flour, sugar, and butter and spread on top of peaches. Sprinkle lightly with cinnamon and nutmeg. Cover with top pie crust and seal edges. Pierce crust with fork. Bake in moderate Dutch oven (350 degrees) for 30-35 minutes.

Peach trees have long been associated with Old Fort Niagara. Many local histories record that an orchard of peach trees stood between the French Castle and Lake Ontario until the ground was lost to erosion in the eighteenth century.

Hallatt and Lipa, p. 33.

White Sauce
Officers' fare

1/2 pint milk
1 tsp butter
1 1/2 tsp flour
1 blade of mace
dash of nutmeg

Take one-half pint of milk and thicken it with the flour. Add butter, mace and nutmeg. Heat gently. Do not bring to a boil. Blend until smooth. Mrs. Child, in *The American Frugal Housewife*, suggested that "If you want to make it very nice, put in a glass of wine".

Mrs. Child also recommended sauce for common use for all sorts of puddings. Elizabeth Simcoe said of eating whitefish caught at Fort Niagara from October until April that "they are so rich that sauce is seldom eaten with them."

Child, p. 65; Innis, p. 81.

Bread Pudding
Officers' & Common fare

1 quart milk
4 Tbl butter
1 lb stale bread
1/2 cup sugar
3 eggs
rosewater
1/2 cup raisins

Scald the milk and set aside. Crumble bread, add sugar and combine. Beat three eggs lightly into a well-buttered baking bowl. Add milk and rosewater (note: rosewater is an acquired taste. Use caution in flavoring with it) and mix. Stir in crumbs and add raisins. Stir lightly until the raisins sink in. Bake (300 degrees) for one hour. As an option, one teaspoon of cinnamon may be used.

Bread pudding was a common and popular English dish which found favor in the New World as well. While no reference to its use at Fort Niagara has been found, it has been included here because of its popularity with British soldiers in North American and because its ingredients were available at the post. Amelia Simmons specified a gill of rosewater in her recipe, flavoring a bit too strong for modern palates.

Simmons, p. 26.

Rosewater
Officers' fare

petals from fragrant roses
French brandy to cover

Fill a clean jar with fresh, fragrant rose petals. Cover with the brandy. Tightly seal the jar and allow to stand for three or four days. Drain and strain the brandy into a bottle and cork well. A modern alcohol also useful for this recipe is vodka, used in place of the brandy.

Rosewater may be purchased from Greek or Indian ethnic food stores. It was a very popular flavoring in eighteenth century English and American cookery.

Simmons, p. 152.

Shrub
Officers' fare

2 quarts brandy
juice of 5 lemons
peels of 2 lemons
1/2 whole nutmeg
3 pints white wine
1 1/2 lb sugar

Place brandy, lemon juice, peels, and nutmeg into a large bottle. Let stand for 3 days. Add wine and sugar. Mix well and strain twice, then rebottle.

Shrub is an officer's drink, its ingredients far too costly for the common soldier. It would be a most suitable refreshment for the officers' mess.

Hallatt and Lipa, p. 47.

Mulled Cider
Officers' & Common fare

1 gallon cider
2 cups brown sugar
6 sticks of cinnamon
2 tsp whole cloves
2 tsp salt

Dissolve brown sugar into the cider. Bring to a boil. Add cinnamon, salt and cloves. Let simmer for 15 minutes. Strain to remove cloves (or place them in a cheesecloth or tea strainer). Serve hot.

Another popular colonial drink served for an "entertainment". Mulled cider was within the means of the common soldier while also a drink fit for his officer.

Hallatt and Lipa, p. 48.

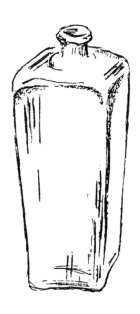

Soldier and Family, Butler's Rangers, 1783

To Feed a Soldier
of the Republic:
1796 - 1815

When United States troops took control of Fort Niagara on August 10, 1796, the young republic was but twenty years old. The movement of even a small number of troops to Niagara caused minor embarrassment to the new nation. A British ship had to be chartered to transport the soldiers since no American vessel yet sailed Lake Ontario. Soon, however, the new masters of Niagara settled in to begin the dreary rounds of repairing the 70 year-old fort.

The logistics of supplying Niagara were difficult for the United States as money and resources were in short supply. American contractors based in Pittsburgh used river and lake routes to maintain the supply line to Niagara. However, the poor quality of flour and its late delivery plagued commandants of the fort. Indeed, the smaller Lake Ontario post at Oswego was even more difficult to supply and suffered badly from lack of provisions shortages. On August 25, 1801, Fort Niagara's commandant, Major Moses Porter, was ordered to "supply that Garrison immediately with a sufficient Quantity of Liquor & Provision." Oswego, it was noted, had "been for sometime past, distitude of any kind of Meat."

The daily ration that the U.S. soldier could expect to receive was specified in 1802 as "one and one quarter pounds of beef or three quarter pound of pork, 18 ounces of bread or flour, a gill of liquor, salt, vinegar, soap and candles." By 1821 the regulations detailed that bread would be placed on shelves and fresh meat was to be "hung out at the back windows on hooks-but not in the sun." A "mess" of soldiers (6-8 men) was to rotate the duty of cook with each man to take his turn. It was noted that this included the musicians as well. The men were to use the "greatest care" in "scouring and washing the utensils employed in cooking."

Perhaps the single, most lasting impact made on American cuisine in the vicinity of Fort Niagara was an invention of the wife of a former sergeant of the garrison, Catherine Hustler. She and her husband, Thomas, opened a tavern in the village of Lewiston following his discharge from the U.S. Army. The Hustlers were good innkeepers and memorable hosts. Midshipman James Fenimore Cooper, who often stayed at their inn, characterized Thomas and "Kate" Hustler in his novel *The Spy* as "Sergeant Hollister" and "Betty O'Flanagan". Kate Hustler produced drinks with a certain flare, adding a rooster tail feather to the beverages and calling them "cocktails".

Included in this section are more tavern-related dishes. These have been drawn from early American cook books such as Amelia Simmons' 1796 *American Cookery*, and *The American Frugal Housewife* by Mrs. Child.

Plain Biscuit
Officers' & Common fare

2 cups flour
1 oz butter
1 egg
1/2 cup milk

Melt butter and add to the milk. To this add the egg and 1 cup of flour. Mix well. Continue to add flour until a bread-like consistency is obtained. Knead until dough is soft. Break into sections and bake for 10 to 12 minutes at 350 degrees. For more modern tastes, you might choose to add 1/2 tsp of baking powder to help the biscuits rise.

Article 27, section 7 of the 1821 *General Regulations of the Army* notes of biscuit making that "In making biscuits or hard bread, the evaporation is about fifty-four pounds. So that the barrel of flour yields but one hundred and eighty-two pounds of biscuits." Niagara's American garrison was allowed to prepare either soft or hard bread. The hard bread was called "plain biscuit". This was made without milk or butter, and produced a hard, cracker-like biscuit known to soldiers of a later generation as "hardtack". This recipe, drawn from Amelia Simmon's *American Cookery*, provides a more tasty, if somewhat less military dish.

Simmons p. 38; Winfield Scott, p. 7.

Ration Soup
Common fare

1 lb beef
5 pints water
vegetables of the season
salt
1/2 lb bread, sliced

Place 5 pints of water to 1 pound of beef in a vessel. Bring to a rolling boil, and skim off the foam. Then moderate the heat. Add salt to taste. Add 1 pound of "vegetables of the season" such as peas, carrots, potatoes, turnips, or beans. Simmer for 1-2 hours. A few minutes before the end of simmering, add sliced bread. Reduce for 5-6 hours. Add water to broth to replace losses before serving.

This ration soup was the standard fare for the common soldier of the Fort Niagara garrison before and during the War of 1812. He was told to add "hard or dry vegetables ... earlier than is above indicated." It was also noted that the meat (or part of it) could be taken out of the soup, but, if this was done he was to add more water! A story told by Corporal Arthur Lyons, a World War One veteran, gives much the same recipe for a soldier's meal of a century later: "Take one pound of meat and add to ten gallons of water and boil. If too thick, add more water."

Winfield Scott, p. 44.

Salmon
Officers' fare

2-3 lbs salmon
3 Tbl butter
1 onion
1 stalk celery
1 carrot
1/2 cup vinegar
2 sprigs parsley
1 bay leaf
8 whole cloves
1/4 tsp pepper
1 quart water

Dice onion, celery and carrot. Melt butter in spider (skillet). Add vegetables and sauté for 5 minutes. Add vinegar, water and spices. Bring to a boil. Let boil 5 minutes and then strain. Keep the liquid (broth) and discard the vegetables. Wrap the salmon in a piece of cheesecloth. Lay in the bottom of a kettle. Cover salmon with the hot broth. Simmer uncovered for approximately 30 minutes. Remove fish from kettle. Uncover and remove the skin before serving. Serve garnished with egg sauce for a more elegant dish.

Carlo, pp. 91-92.

Egg Sauce
Officers' fare

4 Tbl butter
4 Tbl flour
2 hardboiled eggs
2 cups milk
1 Tbl lemon juice
salt and pepper

Melt the butter over a low heat. Add the flour, stirring constantly, for 2-3 minutes. Heat milk separately. Add milk to butter and flour and stir. Cook about 3 minutes or until near a boil. Add lemon juice and diced eggs. Season to taste with salt and pepper.

Salmon was a commonly caught lake fish at Fort Niagara. Isaac Weld, Jr., in his published *Travels* of 1795-97, mentioned that "Lake Ontario, and all the rivers which fall into it, abound with excellent salmon." Faunal remains from archaeological explorations at Fort Niagara show that salmon was consumed here. A New England egg sauce is included to provide a "Yankee" flavor to this local delicacy. Fort Niagara's commandants from 1800 through 1813, Major Moses Porter and Captain Nathaniel Leonard, were both natives of New England. Perhaps they enjoyed their Lake Ontario salmon with sauce from their home states.

Carlo, p. 92; Weld, p. 86.

Fry Meat
Common fare

1 lb beef or 3/4 lb pork

Take ration meat, trim fat away and save. Place fat into a kettle and heat to "hissing hot". Cube meat into bite-size pieces and add to kettle. Fry for 12-15 minutes.

On January 6, 1813, Private Matthew Campbell was tried at Fort Niagara for "striking and cutting Catherine Brown with a knife." It seems that Campbell had used Catherine Brown's wash "kittle" to fry his meat in. When she removed it, he "sized holt of a knife, struck her in the arm and cut her." Catherine reported that "she got the kittle from some person in the yellow barracks and had it for the purpose of washing in." Campbell was convicted and sentenced to "10 cobbs and 2 weeks of hard labour." "Cobbing" was a beating on the behind.

McFeely, pp. 21-23.

Beef and Cabbage
Common fare

1 lb salt beef
2 medium heads of cabbage
salt & pepper
vegetables of the season (onions, carrots, potatoes, or parsnips)

As salt beef is rather too highly impregnated with salt for normal use, fresh beef may be substituted. However, if salt beef is used, soak it overnight in fresh water. Remove beef and discard water. Replace with cold water in kettle. Over a moderate fire (300 degrees) cook for 3 hours, skimming carefully every 15 minutes. After 2 hours, add cabbage (shredded) and vegetables (diced) to fill the kettle. Take out water if necessary to accommodate the vegetables. Boil gently for 90 minutes after adding cabbage. "Vegetables of the season" was an often-used phrase for what to add to soup. Today, any vegetable may be added. For a more historic taste, however, onions, carrots, potatoes, turnips, or parsnips would be best. Normally only one or two of those listed would be available at any time. Season to taste.

"Beef and cabbage" has a long association with the U.S. army of the nineteenth century and is similar to the "bubble and squeak" of Niagara's earlier British garrison. As late as 1862, when Captain James Sanderson published his *Campfires and Camp*

Cooking; or Culinary Hints for the Soldier, this recipe was included. The American garrison of Fort Niagara would have immediately recognized Sanderson's recipe as it was one of their most common meals. Fresh beef was often available at Fort Niagara. Drovers would come from Rochester along the Ridge Road to the Creek Road with herds of cattle. A frequent last stop for the drovers was Colonel Hathaway's tavern in Youngstown which had cattle pens attached. This was located on the site of the Ontario House.

Sanderson, p. 9.

Green Peas
Common fare

1 gill (4 oz) dried peas
mint leaves
1 tsp butter
salt

Place peas in a pot, adding enough water to cover them, but no more. Add a couple of mint leaves and one teaspoon of butter. Boil until peas are tender. Drain water and salt to taste. In her *American Cookery*, Amelia Simmons gave a recipe that makes dried peas edible by themselves. The addition of mint leaves from the herb gardens of Fort Niagara would allow the soldier to eat "pease" and butter without making a stew.

Simmons, p. 89.

Boiled Potatoes
Common fare

10-12 medium potatoes
1 Tbl salt

Place potatoes with skins on into the kettle. Fill with cold water. Add 1 tablespoon salt to water and heat. When the water boils, add 1 pint of cold water to retard the cooking. Repeat 2-3 times with more cold water. When potatoes are nearly done, remove all the water, and stand kettle back into the fire until steam evaporates. Watch closely to avoid burning. Potatoes should be nearly uniform in size to boil equally.

Boiling potatoes over an open fire was no easy task. Captain James Sanderson's *Camp Fires and Camp Cooking* of 1862 details the correct fashion of preparing them. Messing instructions in the 1821 U.S. Army regulations also deal with this soldierly problem. Could it be that the soldier of 1812 had not mastered this basic military task?

Sanderson, p. 10; Winfield Scott, p. 7.

Fried Potatoes
Common fare

4-6 medium potatoes
fat

Cut potatoes into slices or quarters (remember, quarters do not crisp as well as slices) and place in cold water for 30 minutes. In a frying pan, heat fat (pork or beef) until "hissing hot". Add potatoes and fry until golden brown. Drain fat and serve. Shortening maybe used in lieu of fat.

Frying food had always been against regulations in the U.S. Army. General George Washington repeatedly ordered his men to stop this practice, and, of course, they fried anyway. Soldiers at Niagara would almost certainly have shared this disregard for army law in 1812 (as well as in 1846, 1861 and 1898)!

Sanderson, p. 10.

Rum, Brandy, Whiskey, Wine and Cider
Officers' & Common fare

Liquors were plentiful among the officers and men of Fort Niagara's French, British and United States garrisons. An idea of the wide variety of beverages consumed may be obtained from the "Time Line of Foodstuffs" at the end of this book.

Alcoholism was a common problem in armies of the eighteenth and early nineteenth centuries. The pervasiveness of liquor is obvious from official documents and courts martial records of the time. One garrison order from Fort Niagara dated October 12, 1813, stated that "In future no spirit of any kind, either rum, brandy, whiskey, wine, cider, will be permitted to be sold, bartered or in anyway bargained for within this garrison on the bottom or within 100 yards of the barrier gate. No person will be permitted to pass in side the barrier gate with a pail, bucket, campkettle, tin pail or canteen or any kind of cup that can contain spirits without a written permission from the Commanding officer." This order, like many before and after, was often ignored by the common soldier (or officer). All of the beverages listed would have been found with frequency among the hard-drinking members of Fort Niagara's U.S. garrison. The problem of drunkeness was compounded by the fact that whiskey was a ration item in the United States service.

McFeely, p. 93.

Coffee
Officers' & Common fare

whole coffee beans
water
1 egg white
1/2 eggshell, crushed

To Roast Coffee Beans:

Roast the beans in an ungreased roaster or a hanging skillet over hot coals. Stir beans frequently until they are dark and brittle. Grind beans.

To Brew Coffee:

Bring water to a boil in a kettle. Add 1-2 tablespoons of ground coffee per 2 cups boiling water. Adjust quantity for strength desired. Keep coffee near boiling point but do not allow to boil. Cook for 20 minutes. Before you remove the pot from the fire, drop in crushed eggshell and eggwhite. Add 1/2 gill of cold water (to settle grounds). Let stand 5 minutes before serving.

Although drunk by British officers, coffee was noted as the most popular drink of the young American republic. Starting as a drink for officers during the Revolutionary War, it had become a common favorite by the time of the War of 1812. Many substitutes were used when coffee was not available. *The American Frugal Housewife* lists brown bread crusts, rye grain and peas as a few examples. Its author, Mrs. Child, recommended grinding your coffee beans soon after roasting them.

Child, pp. 82-83.

Recipes from the Old Fort

The recipes in the preceding sections are only a sampling of the most thoroughly documented dishes eaten by the French, British and United States garrisons of Fort Niagara during the eighteenth and early nineteenth centuries. The recipes in this chapter are all good and enjoyable dishes, but they do not have the historical context of the other recipes. Many of them have been prepared for years in the Old Fort Niagara cooking program. All include ingredients that were available to the soldiers or officers of Fort Niagara.

One non-period ingredient will be found in a number of these recipes. That is baking powder which is a relatively modern concoction. For modern preparation of the recipes below, simply use baking powder. In order to make them more appropriate for period cookery, you may use, as a baking powder substitute, a mixture of cream of tartar and soda:

2 tsp cream of tartar
1 tsp baking soda
3/4 tsp flour

Soft Molasses Cookies

1 cup sugar
1 cup molasses
1 cup butter and lard mixed
1 level Tbl soda dissolved in 2/3 cup warm water
1 tsp ginger
pinch of salt
4 cups flour

Mix ingredients together. These may be baked as either cutout or drop cookies. Bake on greased cookie sheet at 450 degrees for 7 minutes.

Hallatt and Lipa, p. 32.

Hobnails

1 1/2 cups flour
1 tsp vanilla
1/2 tsp salt
1/2 cup raisins
1/2 tsp baking soda
1 tsp cinnamon
1 cup light brown sugar
1/2 cup lard
1 well-beaten egg

Cream together sugar, beaten egg and vanilla. Add remaining dry ingredients a little at a time. Form into small balls. Place on greased baking sheet about 3 inches apart. Bake at 350 degrees for 12-15 minutes.

Hallatt and Lipa, p. 8.

Eggless Cake

1 cup sugar
2 cups flour
1 tsp soda
1 tsp nutmeg
1 tsp cinnamon
1 tsp ground clove
1 cup sour milk
1/2 cup lard & butter mixed
1 cup raisins, well-floured

Combine dry ingredients. Add sour milk and butter/lard mixture. Mix. Add raisins. Bake at 350 degrees for 30 minutes or until done.

Dutch Oven: Bake in hot Dutch oven until inserted splinter comes out clean.

Hallatt and Lipa, p. 30.

Dutch Oven Cornbread

This recipe for "cornbread" is unique in that it does not use any corn meal. Instead, it is made with regular flour. Surprisingly, it tastes like real cornbread. This will provide the flavor of period cornbread for persons who are unable to eat corn.

1/4 cup melted butter
1 Tbl sugar
3 tsp baking powder (or cream of tartar)
2 eggs
1 tsp salt
1 1/2 cups milk
2 cups flour

Melt butter. Combine dry ingredients in a large bowl. Beat eggs and milk together and pour over dry ingredients. Stir until smooth. Add melted butter, and stir until well mixed. Pour into a buttered Dutch oven. The batter should not be more than 1 1/2 inches deep. Cover. Pile coals in lid and around base of Dutch Oven.
Modern oven: Bake at 375 degrees for 20-30 minutes.

Hallatt and Lipa, p. 9.

Les Croquignoles (Crullers)

4 cups flour
1 tsp nutmeg
1 cup sugar
1/2 cup milk
4 Tbl melted lard
2 tsp salt
1 tsp cinnamon
4 tsp baking powder
4 well-beaten eggs

Combine well beaten eggs, sugar, milk and melted, cooled lard.

Sift together dry ingredients. Mix well with egg mixture. Knead gently. Pat or roll out to 1/2 inch thickness. Cut about 1 1/2 inches long and 1 inch wide. Give a slight twist and drop into hot lard. Cook until light brown, drain on paper and roll in either granulated or powdered sugar. Crullers are best served hot.

Hallatt and Lipa, p. 9.

Bannock

2 lb flour
2 tsp baking powder
1/2 tsp salt
1 Tbl melted lard
1/2 pint warm water

Mix ingredients and knead thoroughly. Divide dough in two, baking one half at a time. Press each half into a greased pan. The dough should touch the sides of the pan and should be about 1/2 inch thick. Prop the pan up so that it is perpendicular to the coals of the fire. Bake until the center is done, about 15-30 minutes. While baking, turn the pan 3 or 4 times and baste with lard. Dip in hot grease or lard when eating.

Bannock is actually a Scottish dish for oat cake. For true Scottish bannock add one-half pound of oatmeal to the flour.

Hallatt and Lipa, p. 19.

Boston Brown Bread

2 cups sour milk
1/2 cup molasses
2 cups flour
2 cups whole wheat flour
1 1/2 tsp soda
scant tsp salt

Combine ingredients. Divide dough and place in two 1-quart buttered pudding molds. Fill each mold 3/4 full. Cover molds with buttered lids. Lids must be secured tightly to prevent lifting. Place pudding molds in pan with water level halfway up the mold. Steam 3 hours and bake 1/2 hour. Coffee cans covered with aluminum foil may be used if pudding molds are unavailable.

Hallatt and Lipa, p. 25.

Sally Lunn

2 cups flour
3 tsp baking powder
1/2 tsp salt
2 eggs, separated
1/2 cup milk
1/2 cup melted butter

Mix and sift the dry ingredients. Add the milk to the beaten egg yolks and add this mixture to the dry ingredients, stirring until just mixed. Stir in the melted butter, then fold in the stiffly beaten egg whites. Bake in a well-greased 9-inch square pan in a moderate oven (350 degree) for about 30 minutes.

The name "Sally Lunn" is believed to have evolved from the French words for sun and moon - "*soleil-lune*". The tops of these buns would turn a golden brown, but the bottoms would remain white. Thus it was thought that they resembled the sun and moon. In England the French *soleil-lune* was garbled into "Sally Lunn". The recipe has also changed. Although originally buns, over the years Sally Lunn has become more of a cake.

Hallatt and Lipa, p. 26.

Raisin Bread

1 package yeast
2 1/2 cups warm water
2 tsp salt
2 tsp cinnamon
1/2 cup honey
2 cups raisins
6-7 cups flour

Mix 3 cups flour with salt and cinnamon. Dissolve yeast in 1 cup warm water. Pour into flour, salt and cinnamon mixture. Mix thoroughly. Add honey and raisins. Alternately add remaining flour and water. Knead dough at least 10 minutes. Set in warm place to rise until dough is approximately twice its original size. Punch down and let rise a second time. Punch down again and bake at 350 degrees for approximately 1 hour.

Dutch oven: Generally, the dough is divided into three loaves when baking in a Dutch oven. Baking time varies from 45 minutes to 1 hour. To test if the bread is done, knock on the bottom of the loaf. If it is hollow sounding, then it is done.

Hallatt and Lipa, p. 27.

Cinnamon Flop

Topping:
1 cup brown sugar
4 Tbl softened butter
1/2 tsp cinnamon

Batter:
2 cups sifted flour
2 tsp baking powder
1/2 tsp salt
1/2 cup sugar
2 Tbl softened butter
1 egg, well-beaten
1 cup milk
peaches or apples

Topping: Work brown sugar, cinnamon and butter until crumbly.

Batter: Sift flour, baking powder, and salt together. Mix sugar and butter in separate bowl until well mixed. Stir in beaten egg. Then add flour and milk. Pour into a greased 9 1/2-inch round pan and sprinkle the topping over the surface. Peaches or apples may also be diced and scattered on top. Fruit may be added to batter as well. Bake in 425 degree oven for 30-35 minutes. Butter will melt during baking so it is best to place a cookie sheet under the baking pan to catch the drippings. Served warm this makes a delicious breakfast bread.

Dutch oven: Bake in hot Dutch oven until inserted splinter comes out clean.

Hallatt and Lipa, p. 29.

Suet Pudding

1 cup chopped suet
1 cup sweet milk
1 cup molasses
1 cup chopped raisins
3 cup flour
1 tsp soda
a little salt

Combine ingredients. Place in a cheese cloth and steam over a pot of boiling water for 2 hours.

Hallatt and Lipa, p. 32.

Pumpkin Pie

2 cups freshly cooked pumpkin
2/3 cup brown sugar (packed firmly)
2 tsp cinnamon
1 tsp allspice
1/2 tsp ginger
1/2 tsp nutmeg
1/4 cup butter
3/4 cup milk
2 well-beaten eggs

Combine pumpkin, sugar, and spices in large bowl. Beat in milk, eggs, and softened butter until fluffy. Pour into unbaked pie shell and bake at 325 degrees for 1 hour.

Hallatt and Lipa, p. 34.

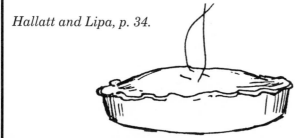

Topping for Pumpkin Pie

1 cup heavy cream
2 Tbl ginger

Add ginger to cream and whip.

Hallatt and Lipa, p. 34.

Chocolate Cake

2 cups flour
2 cups sugar
2 tsp soda
1 tsp baking powder
1 cup baking powder
1 cup baking cocoa
1/2 cup melted butter
1 tsp vanilla
2 eggs
2 cups hot water

Mix ingredients in one bowl and bake at 350 degrees for 35 minutes.

Dutch oven: Bake in Dutch oven for 30-35 minutes. Be careful that coals are not too hot or cake may burn on top or bottom.

Hallatt and Lipa, p. 34.

Nothing Cake

1 1/2 cups brown sugar
1/2 tsp salt
1 cup sour milk
1/2 cup butter
1 egg
2 1/2 cups flour
1 tsp baking soda
cinnamon and nutmeg may be added, if desired, to enhance the flavor

Mix butter, flour and sugar together until crumbly. Take half of the crumbs and set them aside. Add baking soda and salt to the milk. Mix with one half of crumbs. Beat in the egg. Pour batter into greased pan and sprinkle remaining crumbs on top. Bake for about 30 minutes at 350 degrees.

Dutch oven: Bake in hot Dutch oven until inserted splinter comes out clean.

We do not know for certain how "nothing cake" got its name, but it was probably derived for the fact that it contained no fruits, nuts or spices. It is "nothing" special. This cake is a favorite of the men of the Old Fort Niagara Guard. Consequently, they think it is called "nothing cake" because, soon after it comes out of the oven, there is nothing left!

Hallatt and Lipa, p. 35.

Snickerdoodles

3 1/2 cups flour
1/2 tsp salt
1 1/2 tsp soda
1 1/2 tsp cinnamon
1 1/4 cups butter
1 3/4 cups sugar
3 eggs
1 cup walnuts
1 cup raisins

Cream butter and sugar until smooth. Beat eggs and add to creamed mixture. In separate bowl, combine dry ingredients and add to mixture a little at a time. Mix thoroughly. Add nuts and raisins. Drop by teaspoonful onto greased baking sheet. Bake at 350 degrees for 10-15 minutes.

Hallatt and Lipa, p. 37.

Scones

2 cups flour
2 Tbl sugar
1/2 tsp salt
3 tsp baking powder
1 cup milk
1 egg
1/4 cup lard

Mix ingredients. Roll out and sprinkle with sugar and cinnamon. Dot with butter. Cut into small squares. Fold each square in half so that is the shape of a triangle. Bake for approximately 10 minutes at 450 degrees.

Dutch oven: Scones may either be baked in the oven or fried at a low heat using a spider.

Soldier and Officer, US Artillery, 1796

Index of Recipes

...continued...

Soups and Stews

Vegetables

Time Line of Foodstuffs

Listed below are the foodstuffs for which we have found specific documentary or archaeological evidence of use at Niagara or on the Great Lakes - St. Lawrence frontier during the eighteenth and early nineteenth centuries. An "X" in the column under the dates denotes a specific reference to this food during that time period. This allows us to include foods such as milk, barley and cheese, for example, for which a recipe is not needed.

The apparent lack of variety of foodstuffs in the American period (1796-1815) is due more to a lack of available documents than to any sudden shortages. Most of the foods found in the British period were also eaten by their American successors.

Foodstuffs:	1726-1759	1759-1796	1796-1815
Allspice	X	X	X
Almonds			X
Anchovy		X	
Apples	X	X	
Bacon	X	X	
Barley		X	
Beaver		X	
Beef	X	X	X
Biscuits	X	X	X
Black Bass		X	
Blackberries		X	
Bread	X	X	X
Brown Sugar		X	
Buckwheat		X	
Buffalo Tongue	X		
Butter		X	
Cabbage		X	
Catfish		X	
Cheese	X	X	
Cherries		X	
Chestnuts		X	
Codfish	X		
Corn	X	X	X

	1726-1759	1759-1796	1796-1815
Cranberries		X	X
Cream		X	
Crow		X	
Currants		X	
Duck		X	
Eagle		X	
Eel	X	X	
Eggs		X	
Goose	X		
Gooseberries		X	
Grapes		X	
Ham	X	X	
Hare		X	
Herring		X	
Hurtleberries		X	
Indian Potatoes		X	
Killdeer		X	
Lamb		X	
Lard	X		
Lime Juice		X	
Lemon Juice		X	
Lettuce		X	
May Apples		X	
Milk	X	X	X
Molasses	X	X	
Mustard		X	
Mutton		X	
Nutmeg		X	
Oatmeal		X	
Oil		X	
Parsnips		X	
Partridge		X	
Peaches		X	
Peas	X	X	
Pepper	X		X
Pickerel		X	
Pigeon		X	
Plums		X	
Pork	X	X	
Potatoes		X	

	1726-175	1759-1796	1796-1815
Prunes		X	
Pumpkin	X	X	X
Racoon		X	
Raisins		X	
Raspberries	X	X	
Rattlesnake			X
Raven		X	
Rennet		X	
Rhubarb	X		
Rice	X	X	X
Rum		X	X
Rye		X	
Salmon		X	X
Salt	X	X	
Sarsaparilla		X	
Shaddock		X	
Squash			X
Squirrel		X	
Strawberries		X	
Strawberry Spinach		X	
Sturgeon		X	
Suet		X	
Sugar	X	X	
Sweet Peas		X	
Sweetmeats		X	
Tongue		X	
Tortoise		X	
Turkey		X	
Veal	X	X	
Venison	X		X
Vinegar	X	X	X
Watercress		X	
Watermelon		X	X
Whey		X	
Whitefish		X	
Yeast			X

...continued...

	1726-1759	1759-1796	1796-1815
Beverages:			
Brandy	X	X	X
Bristol Beer		X	
Chocolate	X		X
Cider	X		X
Claret		X	
Coffee		X	X
Cordial	X	X	
Eggnog		X	
Flip	X		
Grog		X	
Lemon Punch		X	
London Porter		X	
Milk		X	
Milk Punch		X	
Port		X	
Punch	X	X	
Rum		X	X
Small Beer	X		
Spruce Beer	X	X	
Syllabub		X	
Tea		X	
Whiskey			X
Wine	X	X	X

Glossary

Addled - Spoiled or rotten.

Bateau (pl. bateaux) - A flat-bottomed, double-ended boat used on the lakes and rivers of northern North America by the French, British and Americans for the movement of men and supplies.

Barrel - A large, staved, wooden cask used for the shipment of commodities. The standard weight of the barrels of flour and pork sent by the British to Fort Niagara was 215 pounds.

Bloated - Softened by wilting or steeping in brine, or salted and dried in the sun.

Brine - Water saturated with salt. Used as the most common form of preservative for meat in the eighteenth century.

Dram - (or drachm) A unit of measurement equal to one eighth of an ounce.

Emptins - A form of yeast made from the dregs of beer.

Firkin - Small wooden vessel for butter and cheese, one quarter barrel in measurement. The normal weight of a "Canadian firkin" during the British period was 66 3/4 pounds.

Fricassee - A dish of meat cut small and stewed.

Gill - one quarter of a pint, 4 fluid ounces.

Jerusalem Artichoke - An American sunflower widely cultivated for its tubers. Used as a vegetable and livestock feed. Commonly known as "Indian Potatoes".

Kettle - A commonly used cooking pot of the eighteenth century. A modern substitute would be a saucepan.

...continued...

Pearl Ash - A salt obtained from wood and plant ashes used as an early form of leavening (also called potash).

Ration - The amount of food designated by the army to be issued to one man for one day. An ideal not always meet by the army.

Rice - Rice would have been brown rice, or short to medium grain white rice (for officers), it does not apply to the long grain rice available today.

Rosewater - Flavoring extract made from roses.

Rye and Injun - A mixture of rye flour and corn meal.

Salt beef - Fresh meat preserved in salt water in barrels, improper handling could lead to meat spoilage.

Shallot - A bulbous herb resembling an onion and producing small clustered bulbs, used in seasoning.

Spider - A cooking pan which resembles a modern skillet with the addition of three long legs which allow it to stand over a fire.

Tierce - A large wooden cask used for the shipment of rice and peas during the British period. The normal weight of a tierce was 531 pounds. These containers were frequently damaged in transit up the St. Lawrence River and Great Lakes because of their great size.

Trivet - A flat cast iron piece of metal made in varied shapes, with three legs attached. Used as a base for flat bottomed pots to allow them to be put over the fire.

Whortleberries - a variety of blueberry.

Sources

Armour, David A. and Widder, Keith R. *At the Crossroads: Michilimackinac During the American Revolution*. Mackinac Island, MI: Mackinac Island State Park Commission, 1978.

Benson, Adolph B. (ed.). *Peter Kalm's Travels in North America: The English Version of 1770*. New York: Wilson-Erickson, Inc., 1937.

Bethune, Joanna. *The Unpublished Letters and Correspondence of Isabella Graham for the Years 1767 to 1814*. New York: John S. Taylor, 1838.

Bowler, R. Arthur. *Logistics and the Failure of the British Army in America, 1775-1783*. Princeton, NJ: Princeton University Press, 1975.

Carlo, Joyce W. *Trammels, Trenchers, & Tartlets: A Definitive Tour of the Colonial Kitchen.* Old Saybrook, CT: Peregrine Press, 1982.

Chartrand, René. *The French Soldier in Colonial America*. Bloomfield, Ontario: Museum Restoration Service, 1984.

Child, Mrs. *The American Frugal Housewife*. (1833) Cambridge, MA: Applewood Books, n.d.

Cometti, Elizabeth. (ed.). *The American Journals of Lt. John Enys*. Syracuse: Syracuse University Press, 1976.

Cruikshank, E.A (ed.). *Records of Niagara: The First Settlement*. Niagara-on-the-Lake, Ontario: Niagara Historical Society, 1927.

Cuthbertson, Bennett. *A System for the Complete Interior Management and Oeconomy of a Battalion of Infantry*. London: J. Millan, 1779.

David, Elizabeth. *English Bread and Yeast Cookery*. Harmondswark, England: Penguin Books, Ltd., 1977.

Driver, Christopher and Berriedale-Johnson, Michelle. *Pepys at Table: Seventeenth Century Recipes for the Modern Cook.* Berkeley, CA: University of California Press, 1984.

Duncan, Dorothy. *Serve it Forth!* Toronto: The Ontario Historical Society, Toronto, Ont., 1984.

Dunnigan, Brian Leigh. *Siege - 1759: The Campaign Against Niagara.* Youngstown, NY: Old Fort Niagara Association, 1986.

Frey, Sylvia R. *The British Soldier in America, A Social History of Military Life in the Revolutionary Period.* Austin, TX: University of Texas Press, 1981.

Fisher, Jabez M. Manuscript journal of Jabez M. Fisher, June, July & August 1773. Oneida Historical Society, Utica, NY.

Fitch, Jabez Jr. *The Diary of Jabez Fitch Jr in the French and Indian War, 1757.* Glens Falls, NY: Rogers Island Historical Assoc., 1968.

Flick, Alexander C. "New Sources on the Sullivan-Clinton Campaign in 1779." Reprinted from *Quarterly Journal of the New York State Historical Assoc.,* July & October, 1929.

Forsyth, George. Manuscript account book, 1780, RG 10, Vol. 1838. National Archives of Canada, Ottawa, Ontario.

Gage, Thomas. Manuscript papers of General Thomas Gage, 1759-1775. William L. Clements Library, Ann Arbor, MI.

Grose, Frances. *A Dictionary of Buckish Slang, University Wit, and Pickpocket Eloquence.* London: C. Chappel, 1811. Reprinted as *1811 Dictionary of the Vulgar Tongue.* Northfield, IL: Digest Books, 1971. The 1811 edition was taken almost entirely from Grose's *A Classical Dictionary of the Vulgar Tongue.* London, 1785.

Haldimand, Frederick. Manuscript papers of General Frederick Haldimand, Add. MSS 21661-21892. The British Library, London, England.

Hallatt, Mary Catherine and Lipa, Lynn M. *The King's Bread: Eighteenth Century Cooking at Niagara.* Youngstown, NY: Old Fort Niagara Association, Inc., 1986.

Huey, Paul R. "Animal Husbandry and Meat Consumption at Crown Point, New York in the Colonial Period and Revolutionary War." Unpublished Report, New York State Office of Parks, Recreation and Historic Preservation, Waterford, NY, 1979.

Innis, Mary Quayle (ed.). *Mrs. Simcoe's Diary.* Toronto: Macmillan of Canada Press, 1965.

Kent, Donald H. *The French Invasion of Western Pennsylvania, 1753.* Harrisburg, PA: Commonwealth of Pennsylvania History and Museum Commission, 1954.

Knox, John. *An Historical Journal of the Campaigns in North America for the Years 1757, 1758, 1759, and 1760.* Freeport, NY: Books for Libraries Press, 1970. Edited by Arthur G. Doughty.

Langton, H.H. (ed.). *Patrick Campbell: Travels in North America.* Toronto: Champlain Society, 1937.

McFeely, George. Order book of Lt. Col. George McFeely, 1812-13. Archives of Ontario, Toronto, Ontario. Typed copy of the original.

Parker, Arthur C. "Iroquois Uses of Maize and other Food Plants." *New York State Museum Bulletin 144 No. 482.* Albany: New York State Museum, 1910.

Sanderson, Capt. James M. *Camp Fires and Camp Cooking; or Culinary Hints for the Soldier.* Washington: Government Printing Office, 1862.

Sautai, Maurice. *Montcalm at the Battle of Carillon.* Ticonderoga, NY: Fort Ticonderoga Museum, 1914. Edited by John S. Watts.

Scott, Elizabeth M. *French Subsistence at Fort Michilimackinac, 1715-1781: The Clergy and the Traders.* Mackinac Island, MI: Mackinac Island State Park Commission, 1985.

Scott, Patricia and Scott, Stuart D. Unpublished preliminary listing of faunal remains recovered at Old Fort Niagara. Copy in the Old Fort Niagara archaeological project office.

Scott, Winfield. *General Regulations for the Army.* Philadelphia: M. Carey and Sons, 1821.

Simes, Thomas. *The Regulator or Instructions to Form the Officer and Complete the Soldier.* London, 1780.

Simmons, Amelia. *The First American Cookbook, A Facsimile of "American Cookery", 1796.* New York: Dover Publications, 1984.

Simmons, Amelia. *American Cookery, 1796.* Green Farms, CT: The Silverleaf Press, 1984. Edited by Iris I. Frey.

Sloat, Caroline. *Old Sturbridge Village Cookbook.* Chester, CT: Globe Pequot Press, 1984.

Stevens, Paul L. *A King's Colonel at Niagara, 1774-1776: Lt. Col. John Caldwell and the Beginnings of the American Revolution on the New York Frontier.* Youngstown, NY: Old Fort Niagara Association, 1987.

Stevens, S.K. et. al. (eds.). *The Papers of Henry Bouquet.* 5 vols.; Harrisburg: The Pennsylvania Historical and Museum Commission, 1972-84.

Sullivan, James and Hamilton, Milton W. (eds.). *The Papers of Sir William Johnson.* 14 vols.; Albany: University of the State of New York, 1921-65.

Syfert, Marguerite L. *From the Hearths at Fort Stanwix.* Rome, NY: Fort Stanwix, 1977.

Weld, Isaac Jr. *Travels through the States of North America and the Provinces of Upper and Lower Canada during the years 1795, 1796, and 1797.* New York: Augustus M. Kelly Publisher, 1970.

Wheaton, Barbara Ketcham. *Savoring the Past: The French Kitchen and Table from 1300 to 1789*. Philadelphia: The University of Pennsylvania Press, 1983.

Wilson, Bruce G. *The Enterprise of Robert Hamilton*. Toronto: Carleton University Press, Inc., 1983.

Wood, Emma. *Antique Dinner Recipes for All Seasons*. Mount Vernon, NY: Constantia Books, 1987.

Wright, Louis B. and Tinling, Marlow (eds.). *Quebec to Carolina in 1785-1786, Being the Travel Diary and Observations of Robert Hunter, Jr., a Young Merchant of London*. San Marino, CA: The Huntington Library, 1943.

French Soldiers, 1726

Acknowledgements

During preparation of this cookbook, the authors have relied on the assistance, advice and expertise of a number of individuals and institutions. We wish to particularly acknowledge *Mary Catherine Hallatt* and *Lynn M. Lipa* for their pioneering work with the Old Fort Niagara cooking program and for their cookbook, *The King's Bread*. Guiding Mary Catherine and Lynn in the early days of the program were *Delores* and *Robert Pingitore* who spent much time and effort developing the program and introducing the staff to eighteenth century cookery.

The efforts of other Old Fort Niagara staff members greatly eased the production of this work. Archaeologists *Patricia* and *Stuart Scott* have amassed a tremendous amount of information on the foods eaten by Fort Niagara's garrisons as reflected in the animal remains recovered during a decade of excavation. The Scotts have been assisted by an enthusiastic corps of volunteers and staff, notably *Marbud Prozeller*. Mar also drew many of the illustrations for this work as did *Joe Lee* of Garden City, Michigan. Old Fort Niagara Executive Director *Brian Leigh Dunnigan* compiled much of the original primary source material that serves as the basis for programs at Old Fort Niagara and also aided in the production of this publication. *Candice C. Dunnigan* made helpful comments on the manuscript.

Practical assistance with recipes has come from *Dennis Au* of Monroe, Michigan, an aficionado of the art of muskrat cookery, and from the ladies of the current Old Fort Niagara cooking program who have prepared many of these dishes. Among the latter are *Becky Liddell*, *Sue Linnabery*, *Anne Poole*, and *Lisa Seiwell*. Much assistance has also been obtained from the helpful staffs of *Fort George National Historic Park* in Niagara-on-the-Lake, Ontario and *Historic Fort York* in Toronto.

Bringing *The King's Bread, 2d Rising* to completion was the work of *Harry M. De Ban*, Chairman of the Publications Committee, who is responsible for layout, design and production. Thanks also to the other members of the Publications Committee for their work in making aspects of the history of Old Fort Niagara available to the general public.

British Grenadier, 1759

Other titles
in Old Fort Niagara's
series of publications include:

History and Development of Old Fort Niagara by Brian Leigh Dunnigan (1985).
ISBN: 0-941967-00-X.

A History and Guide to Old Fort Niagara by Brian Leigh Dunnigan (1985).
ISBN: 0-941967-01-8.

The King's Bread: 18th Century Cooking at Niagara by Mary Catherine Hallatt and Lynn Lipa (1986).
ISBN: 0-941967-02-6.

Siege-1759: The Campaign Against Niagara by Brian Leigh Dunnigan (1986).
ISBN: 0-941967-03-4.

Glorious Old Relic: The French Castle and Old Fort Niagara by Brian Leigh Dunnigan (1987).
ISBN: 0-941967-04-2.

A King's Colonel at Niagara, 1774-1776: Lt. Col. John Caldwell and the Beginnings of the American Revolution on the New York Frontier by Paul L. Stevens (1987).
ISBN: 0-941967-05-0.

Old Fort Niagara, An Illustrated History by Frederic Ray (1988 reprint).
ISBN: 0-941967-06-9.

The Gold-Laced Coat by Helen Fuller Orton (1988 reprint).
ISBN: 0-941967-07-7.

Forts Within A Fort: Niagara's Redoubts by Brian Leigh Dunnigan (1989).
ISBN: 0-941967-08-5.